GIANLUCA SPOSITO

The Keys of Legal Rhetoric

A Handbook for Lawyers

intra

Unicuique suum

Introduction

The modern speaker (lawyer) confronts people who were trained in an era strongly conditioned by visuals and speed. However, he is technically incapable, because he is no longer trained to fully and correctly use speech and rhetoric, as well as the visuals which become mere support.

Nevertheless, effective forensic communication cannot be achieved in an extemporaneous fashion or without preliminary preparation: communication has to be shaped by studying rhetoric, psychology, and paraverbal and non-verbal communication.

Knowing and being able to use rhetoric allows you to organize your thinking in a technically valid way and deliver persuasive speech.

Conscious and adequate communication represents an added value of the individual and his social context. It is a necessary asset.

Therefore, this book starts with the study of rhetoric and communication in general, which represents a persistent and inexplicable gap in the training of jurists. These aspects have been astonishingly underestimated if we think of the Greco-Roman origins of rhetoric, which still today play an important role in the work of jurists and therefore knowledge of such origins are a key requirement of all jurists.

The speakers of the XXI century should instead know how to value and use rhetorical thinking according to the teaching of classical rhetoric. And they should know how to be 'persuasive', in a technically and ethically correct way. The goal should be a rational and persuasive argument and not persuasion by seduction.

Reading notes

This book represents a practical aid that will allow the reader to understand classical rhetoric whilst focusing on the needs of modern jurists.

The deliberately practical approach has resulted in necessary simplifications, also on several disciplines' topics (law, linguistics, logic, neuroscience, psychology, sociology).

Note to the English edition

This book is a slightly amended version of the Italian edition ("Manuale di retorica forense", 2020). Special thanks to Jessica Cucchiarini and Callum Poyser for their advice and assistance with the translation, but the final choices (and therefore the final faults) are made by the author: guilty!

1. The pillars of forensic eloquence. The role of classical rhetoric

1.1. "Regulated" eloquence. Organization of the speech. *Lógos*, *páthos* and *êthos*

It was always very clear to the ancients, the distinction between the innate ability to speak in a persuasively effective way, namely to "be eloquent", and the codification of the precepts which one could use to express oneself eloquently. Eloquence could therefore be "spontaneous" or "regulated", as a result of the observation of precepts.

Specifically, the art of rhetoric originated from the need to develop skills and methods indispensable for oratory. Over the centuries, contexts and rules have followed one another, but some basic principles relating first and foremost to the framework of reasoning have not disappeared.

As we shall see, for example, the traditional fine canons of classical rhetoric (the components of the communication act) are extremely current, because they correspond to many abilities required by the speaker today: *inventio* (finding the appropriate arguments), *dispositio* arrangement of the arguments), *elocutio* (style, the way in which something is spoken, written, or performed), *memoria* memory) and *actio* (delivery)[1].

More specifically, functional to the forensic oratory - which is connected, of course, with the judicial kind of discourse in classical rhetoric[2] - were (and are) the specific partitions of the discourse: *exordium* (introduction), *narratio* narration of the facts), *demonstratio* argumentation of one's own thesis and refutation of the opponent's one); *peroratio* (peroration or conclusion).

Again, functional to the discourse of judicial kind was the use of topics. This technique made it possible to search for the most useful arguments to support a thesis, depending on the issue to be addressed.

Topics[3] refers to the theory of places of the argument. The term *topoi* is a metaphor introduced by Aristotle to characterize the "places" where a speaker or writer may "locate" arguments that are appropriate to a given subject. As such, the *topoi* are tools or strategies of invention.

Aristotle built it as a research process to act as a foundation on which to base syllogisms and therefore propose his thesis: it is the technique of argumentation that moves from uncertain but probable opinions. Cicero, then, reworked it and finalized its use in court, transforming it into a handbook of argumentative cues and theoretical-practical recommendations to refer to for the

---

[1] While the first three canons concerned the realization of both written and oral speeches, the last two (*memoria* and *actio*) focused exclusively on orality.

[2] Among the rhetorical genres (corresponding to many types of discourse) proposed as early as the 4th century B.C. and then arranged by Aristotle in the model that became canonical, the judicial one was considered the most difficult. Consequently, those who were expert would have been able to try their hand successfully at the other two (the deliberative, typical of political assemblies; the epideictic, relating to speeches of praise or blame).

[3] From the Greek *tópos* 'place'; then in Latin *loci*.

construction of discourse (and so did Quintilian). Through the *tópoi,* we find all the arguments that can support a speech that (unlike the logic-deductive demonstration - e.g. mathematics) starts, develops, and concludes with questionable propositions.

Topics are therefore a warehouse of arguments, ordered more or less systematically and according to different criteria, which can be used to reflect on controversial theses. The field of topics is therefore not the truth (in Greek *alétheia*) but the opinion (*dóxa*); consequently, its conclusions are not true but plausible.

The lawyer's speech is articulated, following step by step these argumentative schemes, like 'molds' into which the case is poured. The essence of the topical method is, precisely, the identification of the most appropriate mold.

Equally functional to the judicial discourse were the *status causae*[4] (results of *inventio*, like topics), and the order to be given to the arguments (results of *dispositio.*

The forensic speaker had to be gifted with *virtutes elocutionis*, namely specific qualities of ornate speech: *puritas* (lexical and grammatical correctness); *perspicuitas* clarity of speech); *ornatus* elegance of expression); *aptum* harmony of speech - both internal, in the definition of the relationship between the parties, and external, in relation to the subject, the context, the audience). Among all these, *ornatus* certainly represented the widest set of 'tools' (in particular, the rhetorical figures) aimed at giving character and persuasiveness to the speeches in the courts.

With these tools, the forensic orator has crossed the centuries and still connotes his speeches with evident

---

[4] The *status causae* (from *stásis,* 'foothold') is instead the nodal point of the question being judged. Depending on the typology (conjectural, quality or legitimacy), it required the use of a special topical for the construction of the discourse.

rhetorical marks, often only decorative, sometimes with a real argumentative function; in the happiest cases, achieving successful results with words that could not be achieved even with images (but we will return to this topic in the chapter dedicated to visual rhetoric).

The structure of discourse and the arrangement of arguments theorized by the ancient rhetoricians (first of all by Aristotle) has been revisited in more recent times (in the mid-20th century, Perelman was responsible for the revival of rhetoric as a theory of argumentation). The ancient tripartition of *lógos*, *páthos* and *éthos*, the three species of evidence (*písteis*) by which the audience can be persuaded, has found new strength.

In fact, the ancients taught that it is necessary to distinguish between objective evidence (*argumenta*, *logos'* exercises) and subjective evidence (pressure and orientation instruments, based on morality or sentiment). *Lógos* is the rational, logical development of speech; *éthos* indicates the character and credibility of the speaker; *páthos* is the set of passions awaken in the audience (the emotional factor).

Theoretically (precisely, with Perelman) there has been a progressive renewal of the model. Rational procedures have been assigned an uncontested role whereas the ethical components have been left in the shadow and everything that represented *páthos* has even been removed from the techniques of argumentation. This is because 'passions' are irrational and disturbing elements, which hinder the reasoning.

In addition to this theoretical path, there has been a concrete change in the style of forensic oratory determined by the changes in the procedural rules (starting from the end of the 20th century) and by the general rapidity for the management of the caseload of courts. The result has been an eloquence without frills, free from the motion of affections, and based on a strict argumentation of facts, in front of a "judge" who has seen the evidence taking shape (in some judicial systems), apparently needing only logical-ordering expositions. Therefore, full revenge, of the *logos* and the demonstrative rigor, on the emotional aspects.

However, it would be premature to talk about the definitive removal of the *páthos*. Communication is, after all, a complex system with interdependent factors, even in a courtroom. Only the rules can be predetermined, but the contents that will develop are not predictable. Just as the emotional reactions induced by those contents are not predictable (i.e., they are only theoretically predictable).

After all, the emotional part is an integral part of the communicative system; just as emotional involvement is an integral part of any interaction, even at trial.

We are therefore faced with an evolution of the Aristotelian *páthos,* certainly no longer represented by procedures that are by now rather outdated, but by the use of much more shrewd techniques (think, for example, of the visual enthymeme and argumentative fallacies, not only in an oral or written speech but also in a testimony). We will come back to thislater.

The contemporary jurist must therefore be able to recognize this *"páthos* 2.0", certainly less evident and therefore more problematic, through the knowledge (never even started during their training) not only of classical rhetoric but also of psychology and paraverbal and nonverbal communication.

In the meantime, we continue our journey in search of the many elements that classical rhetoric still allows us to use effectively.

1.2. The parts of persuasive speech

As we were saying, judicial discourse uses a specific partition: *exordium* (introduction), *narratio* narration of the facts), *demonstratio* argumentation of one's own thesis and refutation of the opponent's); *peroratio* (peroration or conclusion.

According to Aristotle, only two of these parts (i.e. the *narratio* and the *demonstratio*) are necessary parts of the persuasive discourse while *exordium* and *peroratio* would be merely possible because they are superfluous[5].

1.2.1. The introductory part (exordium)

The aim of the introduction is to make the audience (the judge, the jurors, and common citizens) benevolent, attentive, and surrendering[6].

Among the various *tópoi* of the *exordium*, there is first of all the affectation of modesty (or declaration of inadequacy) that consists of confessing one's own inadequacy and is considered an effective instrument because it tends to evoke sympathy towards those in difficulty. Then there is the declaration of brevity, exemplified by the phrase "I'll be brief", which is used in many speeches even contemporary, and which is particularly risky. Finally, the clarification of the motivations that led the speaker to

---

[5] In particular, the *exordium* could have been missing when the speech was necessarily short, or the speaker needed to enter *in medias res* without delay and with a sudden start.

[6] *Benevolum, attentum, docilem.* There was, however, a precise codification of all the precepts (which differed according to the genre, the occasion and the circumstances of the discourse) relating to the ways in which the audience could be pleased.

write or speak (*causa scribendi*) or even to take on the defense, with a possible and more extensive digression.

A particular type of introduction is *insinuatio*. This involves concealing the thesis that is going to be argued, in supporting the alleged oppositions of the audience, pretending to share their opinions or even prejudices, and then winning them after having gained the trust. To gain sympathy and appreciation, which cannot be explicitly asked for, an operation of real 'insinuation' in the mind of the audience is needed (e.g. "I am not here to praise Caesar but to bury him": Shakespeare, *Julius Caesar*).

1.2.2. Presentation of the facts (narratio)

The *narratio* is the story - true or plausible[7], and persuasive - of the facts. Among the three ways in which rhetorical persuasion is carried out ('*docēre*', 'to inform'; '*commovēre*', to move'; *delectare*, 'to delight'[8]), "to inform" is fundamental and typical of the narration of facts. However, to achieve its purpose, it must also be enjoyable and therefore make itself heard and not boring.

You can choose between *ordo naturalis* (following a precise chronological order) and *ordo artificialis* (artificially

---

[7] The forensic speaker works in the field of *dóxa* (opinion), not *alétheia* (truth), using in his argumentation the enthymeme, which is a form of syllogism that argues starting from premises not absolutely certain but plausible, and produces a conclusion equally not certain but plausible.

[8] "It will therefore be eloquent (...) who in the forum and in civil lawsuits will speak in such a way as to convince, delight and move them. To convince [probare] is necessary, to delight [delectare] is pleasant, to move [flectere] is to win": Cic., *Orat.*, 21, 69. The oratory must inform (*docere*) the audience, gain their favor (*conciliate*) and move them (*permovere*): Cic., *De orat.*, 2, 77, 310.

connecting facts and not exclusively linked to the time datum). For example, in this second hypothesis, you can choose to introduce into the narrative some discordances (anachronies) between the order in which the events happened and the order in which they are told. Therefore, we can start *in medias res* (i.e. with the action already started) and then tell the previous events using analepsis (i.e. flashback); or we can anticipate (i.e. prolepsis) subsequent events that will then be resumed and detailed. The evident characteristic of the *ordo artificialis* is that of breaking down the temporal linearity to divide it into mobile sequences.

Whatever the choice, the *narratio* must nevertheless have three qualities: it must be brief (*brevis*)[9], clear[10] (*perspicua* or *dilucida*) and plausible[11] (*verisimilis* or *probabilis*).

Cicero's work and the related medieval treatises offer an interesting and modern (currently used) instrument to verify the conditions necessary for the completion of the *narrative*. This is a specific topic consisting of a grid of questions which represent 'circumstances' to be taken into account in the exposition of the facts: *quis?* (who?), *quid?* (what?), *cur?* (why?), *ubi?* (where?), *quando?* (when?) *quomodo?* (how?), *quibus auxiliis?* (by what means?)[12]? A

---

[9] It corresponds to "what is necessary and sufficient", avoiding the superfluous (*supervacuum*, which is the *vitium* opposed, precisely, to *brevitas*), and avoiding that an excess of conciseness results darkness.

[10] Clarity is also a quality required of the other parts of eloquence.

[11] A mediocre speaker can make even objectively true facts seem unreliable; whereas a good speaker can give credibility even to facts that are only plausible. Here, of course, there are issues relating to morality and forensic ethics, which cannot be dealt with here.

[12] In journalism, the five "W's" help journalists address the

grid of 'empty' forms, to be filled with the facts of the case to be told.

Cicero[13] also suggests inserting, in the representation of the facts, a more immediate representation of the reality (so-called *mímesis*), whose privileged instrument is the *evidentia*[14]. This is a figure that makes it possible to represent the facts "putting them almost before the eyes of the listener" so that they acquire the evidence and the emotional effectiveness of a direct sensory experience.

Thanks to these characteristics, the *evidentia* is also very effective in obtaining an effect of verisimilitude and to equal what is only caused by images[15].

1.2.3. Argumentation (argumentatio)

Argumentation (proof or *probatio*) is at the heart of persuasive speech or text. It consists of confirmation, that is the main part in which logical arguments in support of an opinion(or claim) are elaborated, and of refutation (also called confutation), that is the part of an argument in which the speaker or writer challenges opposing points

---

fundamental questions that every story should be able to answer.

[13] Cic., *De orat.*, II, 328.

[14] In Greek *enárgeia*: the ability to put the treated fact before the eyes of the public almost at the very moment it takes place. Above all, the Greeks reflected on these problems, mostly related to the theme of imaginative capacity, finding the term *enárgeia* for this expressive competence. They also realized its close links with another similar characteristic which is called - resembling phonographically the word *enárgeia* - *enérgeia* (dynamic expression: Quint., *Inst.*, 8, 88). They often experimented and practiced them both to achieve the *ékphrasis* (this is a vivid, often dramatic, verbal description of anything, person, or experience).

[15] We will return to this topic in the chapter on visual rhetoric.

of view.

The *inventio*[16] consists precisely in the search and discovery of the logical arguments suitable to make a thesis reliable. They consist of enthymemes, i.e. syllogisms whose premises are not necessarily 'true' but 'plausible' to the audience.

The enthymemes consist of one or more premises that are sought in general ideas to form the basis of reasoning. They should be generally accepted ideas and opinions which are part of the collective memory. Therefore, the places where they are located, i.e. the *tópoi,* are used to trace them.

Aristotle's theory of *tópoi* provided a model and a basis for the posterior topics. Cicero reworked it to aim for a pragmatic finalization (the defense in court). He composed a handbook of argumentative ideas and theoretical-practical advice (today we would refer to it as a *vademecum* or manual). Quintilian worked on the catalog of Aristotelian *loci* taking into account the judicial practice developed at that time, resulting in a primary division between the arguments[17] from the person (e.g. the character, the physical aspect, the studies followed[18] etc.) and those from things (e.g. the motive, the circumstances of space and time etc.).

However, it would be impossible to list (let alone deal

---

[16] From the Latin *invenire,* "to find".

[17] The Latin terminology, classical and medieval, led to the indistinct use of *locus* and *argumentum,* as interchangeable (with a metonymic use of both: the seat for the entity located there and vice versa - on metonymy, as a rhetorical figure, instead we will return to the next chapter).

[18] Greed, irascibility, cruelty and so on often bring credibility or take it away (*animi natura*); force is often considered proof of arrogance (*habitus corporis*); what it counts is how each one has been trained and educated (*educatio et disciplina*).

with) here the numerous *loci* introduced by classical rhetoric, and then revisited by subsequent studies, until the 20th century. Nonetheless, we can point out six groups (proposed by Perelman): *loci* of quantity (what is more frequent, believed by most, better and more reliable); *loci* of quality (what is unique, subjective, personal, unrepeatable, better than conventional and collective); *loci* of order (what comes before or constitutes the cause is hierarchically superior to what comes after and constitutes a consequence); *loci* of the existing (what 'is' has greater force than what is only possible); *loci* of the essence (what is typical of gender is superior to what describes gender in an occasional and episodic way); *loci* of the person (what is linked to dignity and autonomy is superior to what neglects these two values).

1.2.4. The epilogue (peroratio)

It relates to the conclusion of the speech or text and can take place in two ways (which Aristotle considered strictly alternative): the recapitulation and the motion of affections.

The recapitulation schematically summarizes the topics discussed and the solutions proposed. It is a reminder of the fundamental points of one's speech.

The motion of affections is the true peroration (*peroratio*) intended to awaken emotions.

However ancient rhetoric does not seem to have developed any codified norms related to the epilogue[19].

------

[19] This topic has instead been dealt with greater attention and interest in the filed of linguistics, which has tried to describe (studying mainly literary works) the rhetorical procedures used to highlight the end of a speech (literary work). This is because - just to

Recapitulation and motion of affections are not real closing protocols. They represent general strategies suitable for a particular communicative contingency and in fact usable in other parts of the discourse, depending on its complexity and length and the consequent need that may arise in other phases.

1.3. Organization of the arguments (*dispositio*)

Dispositio is the part of rhetoric that codifies the strategies to establish the order of a speech (or a text) in its various aspects: to arrange the parts in sequence, to put in order the words within a single sentence, to narrate a series of events in a clear, short and compelling way; or to organize the arrangement of the arguments in support of a thesis.

Concerning the latter, classical rhetoric codifies three possible models that could be used to arrange the arguments.

The first model includes placing a more solid argument at the end of the speech. This is the so-called ascending order. In this way, at the end of the speech, the audience remembers the last and most vivid evidence. However, there is a risk of boring the audience at the beginning and the risk of losing credibility due to the weak initial arguments. In summary, there is a risk of leaving the audience behind.

A second possibility is to present the strongest arguments at the beginning dealing with the weakest ones gradually and in descending order. This model, however,

---

briefly mention - with the epilogue the reader/listener can give form and coherence to the discourse, which no longer appears to him as a series of elements but as an organic design, a complete and even semantically cohesive totality.

makes it more difficult to conceal the less effective arguments. These are placed at the end of the argument and therefore the audience will remember them better and perhaps end up remembering only those.

The third model, called the Homeric order or Nestorian order[20], combines the two previous ones, taking into consideration their positive aspects and avoiding their disadvantages. It deals with the more fragile arguments in the middle of the probative discourse, leaving the more persuasive ones at the beginning and at the end. In this way, the speaker will not risk losing authority or boring the audience and, at the same time, will make sure that those strong arguments that have been left for the final part are memorized by the audience precisely because of their effectiveness[21].

However, there is one more aspect to be considered. The speaker-lawyer should also always take into account the changes in the attitude of the audience caused by the speech. The speaker should be able to recognize and evaluate the changes and gradually rearrange the arguments accordingly. This results in a necessary and permanent adaptation.

---

[20] From the arrangement shaped as pincers with which Nestor, in the fourth book of the Iliad, had deployed the Greek troops in battle.

[21] It was suggested by Cicero (*De orat.*, 2, 77, 313) and Quintilian (*Inst. orat.*, 7, 1, 10).

1.4. The linguistic and expressive form (*elocutio*). The virtues of verbal expression (*virtutes elocutionis*)

Elocutio is the act of giving linguistic form to ideas[22]. It identifies and teaches the strategies to construct a linguistic expression appropriate to the arguments thanks to the *inventio* and placed according to a suitable *dispositio*.

The speaker can rely on two different repertoires: *copia verborum* (the entire lexical heritage of the language) and *copia figurarum* (the repertoire of possible connections between words[23]).

Cicero already indicates four main qualities or *'virtutes'* that the verbal expression should possess (*virtutes elocutionis*): *aptum* (appropriateness), *puritas* (lexical and grammatical correctness), *perspicuitas* (clarity), *ornatus* (elegance).

A speech should first of all be appropriate to the purpose and circumstances (*aptum*). This quality includes the need to choose words that reflect the nature of things (plausible speech) and that does not offend the moral sense of the audience (decent speech).

Following lexical and grammatical norms (*puritas*) ensures the linguistic comprehensibility of the speech. This virtue requires the use of words, syntactic constructs, and expressions compliant with current and possibly specialist usage. When faced with a possible conflict between

---

[22] The *elocutio* has been the topic of countless classifications over the centuries, it is impossible even to summarize them. Certainly, a point of reference (also for figures and rhetorical schemes) is represented by the arrangement of Lausberg (1969) and the related simplification made by Mortara Garavelli (1988).

[23] In Greek *schêma* means 'figure': in fact, these are expressive patterns.

grammar and rhetoric, the latter is preferred (and the typical figures of *ornatus*, which can sometimes force the correct grammatical and lexical order).

Clarity is required (*perspicuitas*) to ensure that the speech is generally comprehensible and defends the speaker's argumentative intention avoiding any misunderstanding. It is first and foremost a reflection of clarity of thoughts (the plan of *inventio* must be reflected in that of *elocutio*). The risks to be avoided include semantic and syntactical ambiguity (particularly active, as we shall see, in argumentative fallacies), as well as the corresponding error which is obscurity. However, please note that it is obscure the speech that is incomprehensible also because it is pronounced with insufficient volume of voice, with a confused diction etc.

The last virtue (*ornatus*) instead codifies the artistic and aesthetic aspects of rhetorical discourse. It represents an important requirement[24], although formally accessory, which over the centuries has been overgrowing to the point of occupying the entire field of the discipline. In recent decades, people talk of "restricted" rhetoric, conceived as a technique of verbal expression or as a catalog of rhetorical figures[25].

---

[24] "Which type of speaker gives men a thrill? Which type of speaker is observed with admiration? Which type of speaker receives cries of admiration? Which type of speaker is considered a god among men? The speaker whose speeches are clear, well organized, copious, with both excellent content and form; the speaker who manages to give an almost poetic rhythm even to the prose. This is the style I refer to as ornamented. The speaker who delivers his speech taking into consideration the importance of facts and people, deserves praise for the type of talent that I call convenience and congruence": Cic., *De orat.*, 3, 14, 53.

[25] It is worth mentioning that over the centuries (especially since the 16th century), there has been an aggravation both of

1.5. The rhetorical skills of the forensic speaker

The Roman forensic speaker represents the *homo sapiens* in the evolutionary path that leads to the modern legal profession. He is not only someone with a deep knowledge of Law, but he is, first of all, an expert in rhetoric, on which he was trained. The evolution of the trial system (with the introduction, in Roman times, of a real 'hearing') has allowed speakers to find a place in the courtrooms[26].

Thus the rhetors became the true protagonists of the Roman criminal trial: in the *forum*, among the stands crowded with spectators (who were also climbing the capitals of the pillars[27]), they demonstrate their oratory skills, meet with the approval of those who, anxiously, are waiting to be fascinated by a gesture or a word.

After all, in Roman times, one of the ways of embarking a political career for a lawyer was to support a cause with so much creativity and charm to make passers-by

---

attempting to catalogue and of paying too much attention to the mere stylistic element or embellishment. This has caused to divert the attention from the science of rhetoric as a whole and to identify rhetoric with the purely external aspect and an end in itself. This has harmed rhetoric so severely that it has led, for example, to the negative meaning of the term 'rhetoric' (which has come to qualify redundancy or what is bombastic), which is still commonly used today.

[26] In fact, since the middle of the second century B.C., *iuris periti* were increasingly and fiercely competing in the courts with *oratores*. Their relationship was complex, competitive and of mutual cultural influence. It is likely that the relationship between *iuris periti* and *oratores*/lawyers was that of "teachers towards their students"; but also the *iuris periti* were inspired by the techniques of argumentation of *oratores* which had rhetorical-philosophical origins (Giliberti 2001).

[27] Tac., *Dialog.*, 38 ff.; Cic., *De orat.* II, II, 82 ff.

stop or to attract them to his speeches. People used to listen to lawyers as they were going to a show: for the pleasure of watching them play their role. This was mainly because the Roman speaker was more like an actor and his speeches instilled a feeling of warmth like acting[28].

Therefore, when one of the elders was going to 'speak', the news was spreading fast across Rome and there were great expectations[29].

Obviously, only a few 'stars' of the *forum* had this indisputable presence[30] and were capable of dominating the 'space' within which they were physically moving in front of the judges and the participants. Indeed, very often, even a mediocre speech which was however supported by the forces of *actio* - that Cicero called "a sort of eloquence of the body[31]" - could be more valid than the best speech that was lacking of *actio*[32].

Thus the *oratores* dominated the scene by taking ownership of that physical 'spacc' through a wise adjustment of each movement[33], but also - necessarily - by mastering the 'space' of memory, in whose places (*tópoi* or *loci*, as we have already seen) the ideas are located and to which they used to look for arguments suitable for the situations and parts of the argument.

The *orator* had to possess a great ability to distinguish

---

[28] The Roman speaker clearly displays his contempt for the actor's own abilities, while naively confessing that he envies them.

[29] Cic., *Brut.*, 43, 158.

[30] It was a real "spectacular eloquence".

[31] Cic., *Orat.*, 17, 55.

[32] "I personally would be willing to say that even a mediocre speech supported by the forces of *actio* will be more valid than the best speech that lacks of it": Quint., *Inst. orat.* XI, 3, 5.

[33] In Quintilian (*Inst. orat.*, XI, 3) the movements of arms and hands are described and interpreted in many details.

the category and species of things, define, classify, connect; thus to be the only one who could acquire the oratory techniques. The main duty of the *orator-attorney* was to succeed convincingly in any case: it is by spending much time at the courts, that the orator learned that persuasive verisimilitude does not necessarily correspond with the truth and, unlike the truth, is never definitive, but always revocable.

Therefore, he had to be ready to set up any 'discussion' and be able to 'persuade'. But this was only possible through dedication and constant learning.

It is of this exact legacy that contemporary forensic speakers are beneficiary, often unconsciously.

2. Rhetorical figures and schemes

2.1. Rhetorical figures and classification systems

Rhetorical figures are discursive procedures: schemes according to which the expression of thoughts can be modeled.

Filled with figures, the speech loses the transparency of pure referentiality, surprises, and disorients producing an effect of estrangement. Thus, the addressee's attention is directed towards the formal aspects and the consequent sense effects, leaving momentarily in the background the primary function of language (that of informing).

Today's classification systems take into account, without doubt, the ancient rhetorical tradition[34] and use its terminology.

The modern systematization which we are referring to here (Lausberg 1969)[35] identifies two general classes of

---

[34] It should be noted that modern studies aim to establish a distinction between the different categories of figures on a more rigorous theoretical basis than that achieved by ancient rhetoric, while also identifying the logical or linguistic procedures that distinguish each type of figure.

[35] The cataloguing carried out in the second half of the 20th century is complex (Arbusow 1963; Lausberg 1969; Fontanier

speech schemes: the figures *in verbis singulis* words are isolated) and the figures *in verbis coniunctis* (words are connected)[36].

The figures *in verbis singulis* are identified in tropes.

The etymology[37] itself shows that it represents a 'turning point' which is communicated through an expression that is 'diverted' from its original content to cover another content.

The figures *in verbis coniunctis* are in turn divided into two groups: the figures of speech (which concern the artificial arrangement of the elements) and the figures of thought (which shape the contents of speech and are real schemes)[38].

The figures are then distinguished according to their generative principles, i.e. according to the different procedures from which they derive. Lausberg identifies them with the four categories of change identified by Quintilian: detraction (*detractio*), addition (*adiectio*), substitution (*immutatio*), permutation (*transmutatio*. For the *verba singula* the only possible category is that of the *immutatio* ('substitution' - the proper term is replaced by a synonym or by a trope).

1977).

[36] Quintilian already distinguishes a first group of figures that work essentially on the meaning of words from a second group which instead influences the arrangement of words (combination) in the text.

[37] From the Greek *trópos*, 'direction'. Quintilian catalogues thirteen tropes (metaphor, synecdoche, metonymy, antonomasia, onomatopoeia, catachresis, metalepsis, epithet, allegory, irony, periphrasis, hyperbaton, hyperbole): Quint., *Inst. orat.*, IX, I.

[38] Also Quintilian believes there is a clear difference between the figures of speech and the figures of thought: if the former consist of a peculiar use of linguistic materials, the latter are independent from their verbal formulation: Quint., *Inst. orat.*, IX, I, 16.

2.2. Classification by speaker's goals

In order to privilege the practical aspect of oratory art, we will proceed with analyzing the single figures and schemes which are the most used in the forensic context. These have been alphabetically ordered according to their 'function' in the contemporary judicial discourse (both written and oral).

We should also bear in mind that rhetorical figures do not take on a secondary role in the procedural discourse (which is structurally dialogical), but rather constitute its essence.

2.3. To accentuate

The accentuation or amplification is the set of procedures, and the corresponding rhetorical effects, which relate to expanding and intensify both the subject matter of a speech (i.e. data, arguments, opinions etc.) and a single expression. The result, according to ancient rhetoric, is the enrichment of ideas and the intensification of emotions.

Lausberg identifies four general types of amplification: *incrementum* (increment), *comparatio* (comparison between one's argument and another highlighting its superiority), *ratiocinatio* (by which one can deduce, without describing it, the validity and greatness of the topic discussed), *congeries* (accumulation).

Below we will define some of the most used rhetorical figures aimed to amplify.

2.3.1. Emphasis[39]

Emphasis relates to highlighting or stressing a term or a phrase by using an emphasized expression, to make it meaningful and intense (e.g. "He is definitely a real man").

Literally, the emphatic statement confirms data, which is already evident, if not sometimes even trivial. The presence of a *surplus* of meaning is usually achieved with phonetic-prosodic[40] and syntactic instruments.

Among the peaks of accent, we have an increase in speed, vocal prolongation, pauses; and all of them can be accompanied by proxemic indexes[41] (e.g. specific gestures[42]).

Syntactically, the emphasis is achieved by using constructions in which one element is highlighted: *"It was the defendant* who declared it immediately". Finally, in writing/transcription, the emphasis is given by using capital letters ("IT WAS THE DEFENDANT who declared it

---

[39] From the Greek *èmphasis*, deriving from the verb *emphàino*, 'show, make visible', and therefore 'exhibition'.

[40] From the Greek *prosody* 'accent, modulation of voice'.

[41] *Proxemics* is a neologism deriving from *prox-* (from *proximus*) and -emics (as in *phonemics*) coined by E. T. Hall (1963). It designates a branch of semiotics that analyzes how different cultures make use of space and spatial distances connected to the interpersonal communicative interaction.

[42] Quintilian speaks extensively about it in the context of *actio* o *pronuntiatio* (*Inst. orat.*, XI). It is the art of declamation, which includes the recitation and modulation of the voice as well as the gesture and movement. The speaker should have known how to speak and manage the speech like a real actor. In short, ancient rhetoric had already identified and formally arranged the communicative function of the gesture, posture and mimicry. All of these elements are currently analyzed in today's anthropological and semiotic studies.

immediately"). Only by using these methods the precise term or expression acquires a broader sense than the literal one.

2.3.2. *Hyperbole*[43]

Hyperbole relates to exaggerating the meaning of an expression, amplifying or reducing its reference to reality to strengthen its meaning and increase, by contrast, its credibility (e.g. "he was dead tired", "he waited an eternity", "this trial lasted a thousand years" etc.). Traditionally, the hyperbole corresponds to exaggeration, which leads to the use of a statement in which the reference to reality is made purposely incredible to intensify the initial expression, up to the maximum or minimum degree, with effects of various kinds, even ironic and paradoxical. It is precisely the improbability of the entire statement that induces the recipient to seek a meaning different from the literal one.

Hyperbole serves to increase or decrease something beyond the truth, but it's a 'lie' that doesn't want to deceive: to achieve it, it's necessary to deform reality, without betraying it.

---

[43] From the Greek *hyperbállo*, 'throw up, overtake'; in Latin (with the same meaning) *hyperbole* and *superlatio*. In ancient rhetoric this figure was considered an instrument of both semantic amplification and *ornatus*.

2.4. To allude

2.4.1. *Allusion*

Allusion[44] relates to referring, indirectly, to an event, data, or a person, without ever mentioning it explicitly. Latin rhetoricians categorized the allusion as a playful variant of the emphasis: the two figures have in common the significance of the meaning and the ability to make people understand more than they explicitly say. Same as for the emphasis, the addressee's task is to recognize the allusive reference by reconstructing the implicit meaning of the figure, drawing from his own wealth of knowledge that he probably shares with the speaker (the so-called common ground). The speaker will appeal to this heritage, true or only supposed, taking the consequent risks, like for other rhetorical figures; i.e. irony.

The allusion (as well as the reticence) thus establishes between the speaker and the listener, between the writer and the reader, a sort of complicity to reveal the 'unsaid'. But what is left implicit undoubtedly increases the communicative force of the speech.

To amplify. *See* **To accentuate**

---

[44] From the Latin *adludo*, 'joke', and therefore *allusio*, 'joking speech'. The term used by Latin rhetoricians is, however, *significatio*, and there are five 'types' or expedients which cause more conjectures: *exsuperatio* or exaggeration, which scales down what has been said; *ambiguum* or ambiguity; *consequentia*, or the enunciation of the consequences of facts that can be deduced; *abscissio*, or the truncation of speech (which leads to reticence); *similitudo* or analogy, which allows you to guess what is alluded to.

2.5. To attenuate

Attenuation is the opposite of amplification as far as the effects are concerned. However, it is considered a sub-species of amplification concerning the ways of achieving the effects. It relates to mitigating or reducing the scope of a fact.

2.5.1. Litotes[45]

It is a figure which affirms by denying the opposite. For example, "it is not small" to say that it is big. Other examples are commonly used in bureaucratic language: "it is not inappropriate", "not without regret", "it is not irrelevant", "the counterpart's thesis is of no value". The procedure is that of the periphrasis (litotes is a form of periphrasis) and the aim is to express in a mitigated way what is meant to be understood and to reinforce its strength (e.g. "Not O.K." means of saying "Completely unacceptable").

In Italian, the expression "meno male" (literally "less bad") is similar to the English expression "So much the better", used to comment that a situation is more desirable than it is negative (cf. Winston Churchill's comment, since transformed into a snowclone, that "democracy is the worst form of government except for all the others").

Often litotes is a euphemistic periphrasis, in which the harshness of an expression is softened (e.g. "he's not a genius" instead of saying "he's stupid").

However, the effect is often ironic. Precisely, litotes does not have its own specific form but rather represents a formula of passage between different rhetorical

---

[45] From the Greek *litòtes*, 'simplicity'.

schemes combined in a single verbal segment. For example, with the expression "he is not an Adonis" we do not simply mean that a subject is not particularly beautiful, but rather that he is ugly. Thus, litotes approaches irony (and more precisely the irony of dissimulation). In addition, if the affirmation of the contrary becomes superlative, the figure also comes close to hyperbole. After having analyzed the context, the addressee's tasks will then be, to attribute to the expression a value of mitigation, interpreting it in a euphemistic sense; or a value of reinforcement, interpreting it in an emphatic or hyperbolic sense.

This is also why we sometimes speak of a 'two-faced' figure, with which we can achieve both amplification and attenuation.

The litotes is therefore characterized by this decisive responsibility of the addressee in attributing to the expression one of the possible effects (euphemism, hyperbole, irony). Its function will therefore depend from time to time on the argumentative development of the discourse, the context, and the ability of the addressee (to know the circumstances of relevant realities).

It is important to note that with the hyperbole we can evoke a paradoxical limit which is just beyond the threshold of what it is possible (the improbability or absurdity of it leads the addressee to divert his attention from the literal data and guide it towards the threshold of what is possible). Whereas with the litotes the limit is evoked only to be immediately denied. It acts as a catapult for the speaker to guide the thoughts as they desire.

2.5.2. *Euphemism*[46]

It is a form of dissimulation used to replace a direct expression (but considered indecent, dangerous, or offensive) with an indirect, harmless and neutral expression (e.g. "he had a *financial setback*", "he had an *incurable disease*", "he has moved to a *better life*"). Bureaucracies frequently spawn euphemisms intentionally, as doublespeak expressions. For example, in the past, the US military used the term "sunshine units" for contamination by radioactive isotopes).

Sometimes, in writing/transcription euphemism (i.e. verbal censorship) is expressed through an omission of the term to be avoided, and it is conveyed graphically by using suspension dots three, always, and only), similarly to what happens (graphically) when using the different rhetorical figure of reticence.

2.6. To compare

The comparison[47] brings together two or more objects based on a common quality (i.e. "as dumb as a fish"). It is a figure of analogy (like the metaphor, which is a condensed analogy) and includes two very distinct figures, comparison and simile.

---

[46] From the Greek, 'speak well'. The euphemistic periphrasis has origins rooted in inhibitions, decency, good manners and respect for other people's sensibilities. Another element which, not only historically, triggers verbal censorship by appealing to alternative expressions is fear (linked to sacred conceptions of the power of the word: for example, the fear - at certain times and cultures - of evoking evil influences by naming the feared being).

[47] From the Greek *parakonáo*, 'sharp, sharpen'.

2.6.1. Comparison

In the comparison the comparison between two objects is reversible, which means that the two terms can exchange roles without unacceptable consequences from a grammatical, semantic, or logical point of view (e.g. "The tree was as tall as the house" - "The house was as tall as the tree").

2.6.2. Simile[48]

In the simile, the comparison between two objects is irreversible, which means that the two terms cannot exchange roles without unacceptable consequences from a grammatical, semantic, or logical point of view (e.g. "This regret weighs like a boulder"; "This boulder weighs like a regret", which is not acceptable from a logical point of view).

2.7. To oppose

2.7.1. Antithesis[49]

It relates to the juxtaposition of ideas expressed by matching words (or segments of text) with opposite or contrasting meanings, in other words, conceptual polarities more or less clear: for example, the use of the concepts of life/death, beautiful/ugly etc.

However, the opposing terms must have a common aspect or refer to the same semantic field.

---

[48] From the Latin *similis*; in Greek *parabolé* ('comparison').
[49] From the Greek *antithesis*, 'contraposition'.

2.7.2. Oxymoron[50]

It relates to joining two words or expressions whose meaning is incompatible, as they indicate an antithesis or opposition. As a form of antithesis, the oxymoron unites, by opposing them, two thoughts or two meanings that are incompatible because one expresses the opposite of the other. For example, "deafening silence", "hot ice", "learned ignorance", "eloquent silence", "disgusting pleasure", "illustrious unknown", "lucid madness". Shakespeare heaps up many more oxymorons in *Romeo and Juliet* in particular ("Beautiful tyrant! fiend angelical! Dove-feather'd raven! wolfish-ravening lamb! Despised substance of divinest show!" etc.) and uses them in other plays (e.g. "I must be cruel only to be kind" - *Hamlet*, "fearful bravery" - *Julius Caesar*, "good mischief" - *The Tempest*).

The oxymoron differs from the antithesis because it shows a paradoxical coincidence (and coexistence) between opposing terms instead of emphasizing the differences[51].

In the oxymoron two ideas that are normally kept apart because incompatible, are therefore brought together to produce an unexpected short circuit that results in a surprising 'energy of meaning' that strikes the listener or the reader.

It is therefore a game of intelligence whose main

---

[50] From the Greek *oxýmoron*, 'sharply mad, wittily foolish' (from *oxys*, 'sharp', and *moros*, 'mad').

[51] The oxymoron is very frequent especially in the literary tradition since the classical age ("a discordant symphony" - Horace). In the mid-twentieth century the use of oxymoron in literature widened especially in the titles and from here more and more widely in the titles of media products, until reaching the political world.

ingredient is surprise.

Currently, the oxymoron is frequently used in the language of advertising, politics, and political propaganda but also in very widespread expressions.

In short, the oxymoron has become widely used, in any context.

2.8. To create

Numerous rhetorical figures make it possible to create and convey particularly complex meanings.

2.8.1. Metaphor

It is the most well-known and, at the same time, the most difficult rhetorical figure to define. A conventional definition categorizes it as the replacement of one word with another whose literal meaning bears some resemblance to the literal meaning of the word replaced (e.g. "George is a lion", i.e. he has the courage of a lion)[52].

---

[52] According to Aristotle, metaphor is an elliptical analogy or abbreviated comparison, and brings together different fields of reality (human and animal, natural and artificial, animated and inanimate), making unexpected and surprising similarities visible. And the greater the difference between the images, the stronger and bolder the metaphor and its effect on the audience.

Of this figure (as of others), Latin rhetoricians appreciated the beauty and the ability to capture the attention of the audience, reviving it. However, at the same time, they feared its darkness and improbability, which they considered potentially harmful to the general understanding and credibility of the discourse. It was suggested, therefore, to use this figure with caution (the similarities, for example, should not be too 'distant') and to accompany it with

The metaphor can therefore identify unprecedented links between different aspects of reality. Furthermore, between the cognitive value of the figure and the aesthetic pleasure that derives from it, there is a direct relationship. We enjoy metaphors because they make us discover a state of things that is not evident to us or that we do not think about. Metaphors can be compared to a piece of art: they represent the iconic consideration of the conceptual representation and they link intellectual speculation with the sensitive world.

With regards to the legal field, there are some expressions to be considered metaphorical: "*in limine litis*" ("on the *threshold of* the dispute", in terms of the duty to oppose exceptions or formulate petitions in the introductory acts of the judgment); "*vigilantibus, non dormientibus iura succurrunt*" ("the law assists those that are vigilant with their rights, and not those that sleep there upon", in terms of deadlines for the completion of procedural acts); "*sero venientibus ossa*" ("those who arrive late are left with the bones", which alludes to the fact that creditors who intervene late in the expropriation, participate in the distribution of the sum obtained only after the creditors have been paid on time); "*pro domo sua*" ("for his house", when unbiased arguments are made).

---

attenuating phrases (*ut ita dicam*).

The original Aristotelian theory of the substitutive or comparative conception has been the object of subsequent critical revisions, and more generally the metaphor has been the subject of numerous studies, which cannot be mentioned here, also from a linguistic point of view (in its syntactic, semantic, logical and pragmatic aspects).

2.8.2. Metonymy[53]

According to the rhetorical tradition, it can be achieved when an entity is defined by the name of another entity which is to the first as the cause is to the effect and vice versa, or to which is linked by mutual dependency (container/contents: "the White House" or "The Pentagon" are used to refer to the U.S. presidential staff or the military leadership, respectively; instrument/who uses it: "he has a good pen" means that he is a good writer; producer/product: "drink a Martini"; effect/cause: "listen to Mozart" etc.), with an expandable scope.

2.8.3. Synecdoche[54]

It relates to expressing one notion utilizing another that is with the first in a quantitative relationship.

There are two types of synecdoche. In the first one (generalizing synecdoche) 'the more for the less' is mentioned, which means that the wider concept is used to indicate the more restricted one (the 'mortals' to indicate men, 'America' to indicate the United States of America, the 'iron' to indicate the gun).

The second type of synecdoche is the opposite of the generalizing one and it is called the particularizing synecdoche; through which one mentions 'the least for the most', i.e. the narrowest concept to indicate the widest one (the part referring to the whole: referring to a person by mentioning a single characteristic, "gray beard" meaning an old man; the container referring to its contents:

---

[53] From the Greek *metonymia*, 'name change'.
[54] From the Greek *synekdoché*, from *sýn* 'together' and *déchomai* 'receive, take'.

"He hit the bottle", to refer to his drinking large quantities of liquor etc.).

Synecdoche does not derive from individual processing but rather from a linguistic use which is regulated by cultural customs, and - like metonymies - they constantly influence the language, to the point of modifying the very system of the language enriching its lexicon.

2.8.4. *Periphrasis*[55]

It relates to defining an object not by the term that usually denotes it but by using a circumlocution which indicates certain qualities of the object as a whole, according to a procedure similar to that of the definition.

However, unlike the definition (which makes explicit the essential properties of the object to be defined), the periphrasis highlights the only data that the speaker considers crucial concerning the general context of his communication and argumentative intention.

Periphrasis is a rhetorical device to be used together with different figures (euphemism, litotes, metaphor, synecdoche, metonymy) and has some typical functions. It is used as an instrument of verbal censorship and mitigation, useful to distance yourself from realities (which in any case are 'told') to which is appropriate or necessary not to address explicitly. They may, for example, concern sex, pain, death, or potentially 'difficult' issues.

More simply, its stylistic function is undoubtedly to avoid the repetition of a word already used.

---

[55] From the Greek *períphrasis*, 'turn of phrase'.

2.8.5. *Antonomasia*[56]

It is a form of periphrasis which requires equivalence between the proper name of an individual and certain qualities of the individual. It represents, therefore, an equivalence between the whole and a part of it, similar to the result achieved by the synecdoche, of which it is considered a variant applied to proper names.

It can relate to replacing a proper name with a periphrasis or an epithet, or - on the contrary - in replacing a common name with the proper name of a character who has distinguishing qualities designated by the epithet (e.g. "a Judas", to mean a traitor; "il Duce" for Benito Mussolini; "The Bard" for William Shakespeare)[57].

The greater the cultural correspondence and adjustment between the speaker and the audience the more effective this figure is. Furthermore, antonomasias often represent stereotypes and are particularly influenced by the historical and cultural context and can originate and spread rapidly. They are therefore rapidly used, especially thanks to the journalistic language, and are destined to be forgotten in a few years.

---

[56] From the Greek *antonomasía* (*antí-* 'against, instead of' and ónoma 'name').

[57] In classical rhetoric, the antonomasia is an instrument of amplification, used mainly for the realization of epideictic speech, and can be combined with other figures (such as emphasis, irony, allusion, quotation, metaphor). But in addition to *amplificatio*, the antonomasia can be functional to *variatio* (because it allows to avoid the repetition of a proper name) and also to the rules of the *aptum* (which prohibit some names considered taboo - think of Satan, also known as "the Evil One").

2.8.6. *Synesthesia*[58]

It is a type of metaphor that relates to associating terms that belong to different sensory spheres: visual, auditory, olfactory, tactile, and taste. Two different sensory perceptions merge to result into a new and expressive powerful image.

"Rough voice", "sweet scent", "warm color": the two terms refer to different types of sensations such as touch and hearing, taste and smell, touch and sight. These combinations create a sense of alienation and produce the same effects as some rhetorical figures not only like a metaphor but, in certain aspects, also like an oxymoron (as the words are incompatible from a sensory point of view).

Well known since ancient times, the 'phenomenon' was not classified among the discursive technical terms but referred to a specific multisensory mental experience that relates to the ability to interpret a given sensation based on the sensation from another source[59].

To defining. *See* **To explain**

2.9. To digress

The discourse, like any 'path' (using a spatial metaphor), can lead to different stages, which are linked to the argumentative intention of the speaker.

---

[58] From the Greek *synaísthesis*, 'simultaneous sensation' (from *syn-* 'together' and *aisthànomai* 'perceive').

[59] For example, Pythagoras associated numbers and sounds and Aristotle compared tastes, colors and sounds with touch.

2.9.1. *Digression*[60]

It relates to the presentation of topics that are accessory, external or marginal concerning the subject matter, and yet useful for the full understanding of the speech or for the entertainment of the audience (to relieve fatigue or avoid boredom)[61].

The digression does not have a fixed place in the speech, but it is defined as 'mobile'[62].

There are many linguistic signals that are used to introduce a digression: "incidentally", "in brackets", "by the way" etc.[63].

---

[60] In Latin, *digressio* (or *egressio* or *excursus*), from *gradior* ('walk') and therefore 'distance from a path'.

[61] "Lawsuits are made not in the interest of clients, but so that lawyers can perform there" Quintilian tells us in a passage where he justifies the introduction, in the forensic field, of 'spectacular' eloquence (also consisting of digression, for the pleasures of rhetoric - the latter therefore also appears related to the concepts of 'transgression' and 'entertainment'). After all, a too dry discourse, made up of a rapid narration and too narrow arguments, would risk appearing cold and, therefore, ineffective (Quint., *Inst. orat.*, IV, 3, 2).

[62] Classic rhetoric admits that this 'violation' of the *dispositio* of discourse occurs mostly between narrative and argumentation. But the speaker will have to justify the use of this element either by referring to the overabundance of the subject matter (which at a certain point can no longer be contained in the intended tracks - Cic., *De orat.*, II, 312) or by giving the impression of being driven by passion outside of the natural order of the speech, forced by an emotional impulse to abandon the drawn path (Quint., *Inst. orat.*, IV, 3, 5).

[63] An homologous linguistic signal in English, "*by the way*", fully shows the spatial metaphor of discourse as a 'path', 'itinerary', and how the digression represents a variation of it.

2.9.2. *Parenthesis*[64]

It designates both the graphic signs and the parts of text between them. The rhetorical figure involves the insertion of a syntactically independent verbal segment within a statement.

Parenthetical statements may have an explanatory or additional function and are accompanied by prosodic signals (intonation and intensity of voice) or, in writing/transcription, by graphic signals (hyphens, commas, parentheses).

They can be used to create very complex argumentative strategies (e.g. they can be used to split the discourse into two parts to make them deliberately opposing, to give the discourse an ironic effect etc.).

2.9.3. *Prosapodosis*[65] *or subnexio*[66]

It is the annexation of one or more ideas to a theme already developed. It relates to the comparison (i.e. the development of an antithesis which results in the opposition of two concepts compared, in addition to the theme already developed) or in the etiology[67] (which illustrates point by point the causes and origins of some considerations previously stated or the multiple reasons for a single statement).

More than a real rhetorical figure, it can be considered

---

[64] From the Greek *parénthesis* 'insertion' (from *parentíthemi*, 'insert').

[65] From the Greek *prosapódosis* (from *prosapodídomi* 'I add, I determine').

[66] From *subnecto* 'I add'.

[67] From the Greek *aitiología*.

a mechanism of discourse, through which to organize thoughts in a hierarchical form[68].

2.10. To query

The *rhetorical question* is a question that does not expect any other answer than the (obvious) confirmation of what is being questioned. It is therefore not a request for information, and it is a mandatory answer (yes or no - e.g. "Isn't all of this extremely boring? [Of course, it is!]")[69].

---

[68] This was already the opinion of Quintilian, rather skeptical in defining it among the rhetorical figures: "It is called *prosapòdosis*, and it must be observed as much as possible in the case of several statements. This is because either the reason is immediately followed to the individual points, as in Gaius Antony: "But I do not fear him neither as an accuser, because I am *innocent*, nor as rival, *because I am Anthony, nor do I* expect him to become consul, *because he is Cicero*", or, after having introduced two or three affirmations, he gives the reasons in the same order and without interruption, as in Brutus about the dictatorship of Gnaeus Pompey: 'It is better not to command anyone than to be a servant of someone, because one can live honorably without commanding, while there is no life in a state of slavery'": Quint., *Inst. orat.*, IX, 3, 93-95.

[69] The classic example of a rhetorical question is undoubtedly represented by the beginning (*exordium*) of the first of Cicero's speech against Catiline (four orations spoken in the Senate in 63 B.C. following the discovery and repression of the conspiracy that belonged to Catiline). Configuration of questioning that even reaches the tone of the invective: "When, Catiline, are you going to cease abusing our patience? How long is that madness of yours still going to mock us? When is there to be an end of that unbridled audacity of yours, swaggering about as it does now? Do not the nightly guards placed on the Palatine Hill - do not the watches posted throughout the city - does not the alarm of the people, and the union of all good men -does not the precaution taken of assembling the senate in this most defensible place - do not the

The question can, however, take different forms: *dubitatio*, *sermocinatio* and *percontatio*, which we will examine individually.

2.10.1. Dubitatio[70]

It is the rhetorical figure represented by the question to oneself. Uncertainty is manifested between two or more possible interpretations, examining conflicting circumstances and opinions, weighing the pros and cons, in order to make a decision.

2.10.2. Sermocinatio[71]

Here the speaker or the writer reports a monologue or an intellectual reflection of his or her own or belonging to

---

looks and countenances of this venerable body here present, have any effect upon you? Do you not feel that your plans are detected? Do you not see that your conspiracy is already arrested and rendered powerless by the knowledge that everyone here possesses of it? What is there that you did last night, what the night before - where is it that you were - who was there that you summoned to meet you - what design was there which was adopted by you, with which you think that any one of us is unacquainted?". A pressing sequence of rhetorical questions, ending in the famous exclamation "O tempora! O mores!".

A construction also enriched by the use of other rhetorical figures, such as the anaphora (through the repetition six times in a row of *nihil* - 'nothing' - within the fourth rhetorical questioning) and the homeoteleuton, that is the repetition of several words with the same ending (in this case *egeris, fueris, convocaveris, ceperis*), which gives an even tighter and more pressing rhythm.

[70] 'Hesitation' (in Greek *aporía* 'difficulty, uncertainty').

[71] From the Latin *sermocinari* 'to converse, to discuss'.

another person, containing questions addressed to himself or herself (in essence, we pretend to be asked questions and we answer them - e.g. "Some of you might ask me why we are dealing with this topic in this way").

This form of dialogue can also present itself as the fiction of a dialogue between two or more people, with questions and answers (e.g. "-What do you know?- -I know that I don't know-, Socrates answered him").

When the *sermocinatio* imitates the language, the style, the way of expressing of the character to whom the speech is attributed, it takes the name of *ethopoeia*[72] (or *fictio personae*, as said Quintilian).

2.10.3. Percontatio[73]

It relates to asking questions to others (your opponent or the audience - e.g. "Who among you has never feared for their own safety in such an environment? Of course, all of you!").

The mock questions that the speaker asks include observations of the opponent against which he immediately makes his objections, in the form of an answer (e.g. "-Does the crime require specific intent?- But there is no such thing here! -Does it fall in another case? - And where does it fall?").

2.11. To dramatize

In rhetoric, it relates to inserting in the speech elements

---

[72] From the Greek *ethopoiía* (composed of *éthos* and *poiéo* 'do, create').

[73] 'Interrogation'.

that make the narrator's voice heard, elements that transform him into an actor.

Dramatization can take place using apostrophes and exclamations, but also through questions (*see* **To question**).

2.11.1. *Apostrophe*[74]

Its name derives from the gesture of the speaker who, ceasing to address his audience (metaphorically turning his back), addresses a new interlocutor, usually the opponent (or some other person in the room - but it can also be directed to abstract or collective entities).

Through the apostrophe, the speech undergoes an abrupt change both linguistically (with a change to the imperative or vocative form), and in the point of view and focus of the speech, as well as in the tone (the degree of emotional intensity is greater).

2.11.2. *Exclamation*

There is rhetorical exclamation when an assertive statement is given an exclamatory value through punctuation, pronunciation, intonation or volume of voice. In other words, a 'transformation' of the statement is carried out, leaving its propositional content unchanged (the verbal

---

[74] From the Greek *aprostrophé* (from *aprostrépho*, 'turning away'; in Latin then *aversio*). In the classical rhetorical tradition it was usually performed in the form of an exclamation and aimed to express the speaker's emotions in an obvious way, with the intention of awakening the *páthos* and, consequently, a sympathetic reaction from the audience (so-called *movère*).

formulation and the thematic development) but pro-foundly modifying its meaning thanks to the differential of the communicative function impressed (which therefore it is different from the simple assertion). The speaker intends to show and impart his audience a very different degree of emotional closeness to the subject debated[75].

To eliminate. *See* **To Subtract**

To emphasize. *See* **To accentuate**

2.12. To mask

2.12.1. Simulation and dissimulation

Simulation and dissimulation are figures (attitudes or patterns of thought) that are contrary and complementary to each other. The first (similar to irony[76]) relates to

---

[75] Furthermore, classical rhetoric poses the questioning and exclamation among the functional figures of *amplificatio*.

[76] Furthermore, in ancient rhetoric there was a figure called "simulation irony ", a form of confutation used very frequently in Socratic dialogues. Since Socrates declares his 'not knowing', none of the confutations he makes can be based on the opposition of his own truth (which Socrates recognizes he does not possess) to the truth of his interlocutor. How then can one demonstrate the falsity of a statement without opposing it with a true one? Socrates applies a method of discussion that relies only on what the interlocutor affirms, accepts and recognizes. After asking the interlocutor to declare explicitly and clearly on what he 'believes to be true', he proceeds by showing all the possible consequences of the interlocutor's thesis, and highlighting them in a broadly

pretending to support a thesis different from one's own, seemingly sharing the opponent's position to awaken first in the audience an emotional reaction of surprise and opposition, and then to highlight the weaknesses and to present the unacceptable consequences, even going so far as to ridicule the interlocutor himself[77].

On the contrary, there is dissimulation when the speaker hides (dissimulates) his thoughts through a systematic use of the figures of attenuation (litotes, in particular) or uses interrogative formulas showing apparent uncertainty (and thus dissimulating his own conviction - so called Socratic irony).

However, dissimulation can also be achieved in other

---

unreasonable sense. These consequences were not explained by the interlocutor, and therefore this demonstrates the irrationality of the initial thesis, and 'ridicules' the interlocutor himself.

[77] In the legal argument, the ridicule has similar functions to absurdity in the logical-mathematical demonstration: reducing to the ridiculous is the same as reducing to *absurdity* (*reductio ad absurdum*). Furthermore, it relates to momentarily accepting the 'principles' of the thesis opposite to the one we want to defend, in order to reject its conclusions as absurd, and thus deny the admissibility of the thesis itself (for inconsistency between the stated premises and the conclusions). The argument for absurdity can also take two different forms depending on whether one wants to prove the truth or simply the falsity of a given proposition. The reduction to absurdity (*reductio ad absurdum*), which proves the falsity of a proposition by showing the false consequences to which it logically leads, differs from the demonstration *per absurdum*, called proof by absurdity (which proves the truth of a proposition with the false consequences of its contradictory nature) . There is great affinity between the two forms of argument: the only difference is that with the proof by absurdity the contradictory proposition is hypothetically assumed, which does not occur in the reduction to absurdity. The latter, on the contrary, represents ultimately the other part of the proof by absurdity, i.e. the syllogistic deduction of the false proposition.

ways, for example by using "sliced modesty", through which the speaker makes (simulates) a (fake and ostentatious) *deminutio* of his authority, skills or the validity of his opinion.

The category of these simulated forms of humility (and *understatement*, we might say) also includes the *"pluralis modestiae"* or the impersonal form or other formulas that replace the first person ("the writer", "the speaker", "the author of these notes").

2.12.2. Antiphrasis[78]

It is the essential and more open form of irony, limited to a single expression in which someone says something but means the opposite (e.g. "What a beautiful day!", while it's raining heavily).

It is therefore based on an extremely simple and visible inversion mechanism, relying on the immediate contextual disambiguation.

The change of meaning can concern both the propositional part ("He has some brilliant ideas", meaning that the ideas are trivial), and the strength given to even a single expression ("Try it!", in the sense of challenging; "Congratulations!", in an ironic sense).

---

[78] From Greek *antíphrasis* (da *antí-* 'against' e *phrázo* 'point, make it clear').

2.12.3. Irony[79] and sarcasm

It is a more complex, subtle, and vague form of antiphrasis (i.e. semantic inversion), which relates to saying the opposite of what one believes and what it really is, but in such a way as to explicitly state one's intention, i.e. to allow the audience not to understand the thesis the speaker intends to support.

Irony is the art of striking without really striking, hiding to cleverly attack, according to the norm of the fox ('ironic' animal, i.e. simulator by nature). It is a sword that wounds but does not kill, and yet it can hurt more than a direct insult.

The possibility of the interlocutors to reference shared knowledge and evaluations, basic assumptions, and expectations on the actualized communicative situation are decisive to trigger the ironic discourse (and its understanding).

Creating an ironic message implies therefore the awareness, by its author, of why it is used, the context in which it is proposed, and the audience for which it is intended, who must be able to accept and understand irony and the message brought (and must therefore share with the speaker a 'common ground ' of knowledge and skills). It is also argued that ironic statements are 'echoic' representations of one's own opinions (self-irony) or those of others. Through irony the speaker reproduces (almost making them 'echo') a vision of the world, to express his or her own position (of distance, disapproval or derision).

Some non-verbal signals have a decisive role in ironic communication: prosodic (the so-called ironic intonation), mime and proxemics. These signals can be

---

[79] In Greek *eironèia*, 'dissimulation, feigned ignorance', which in Latin becomes *simulatio*, 'simulation'.

integrated and can precisely identify an ironic message, favoring the addressee. It is important to note that the addressee must be able to understand it. Irony is a rhetorical figure that requires a specific type of understanding and autonomy, which are dissolved when the explanation of the ironic message is given[80]. As soon as you add a word of explanation, the irony is destroyed.

Irony is certainly different from lying because the intentionally false statement is used to communicate something that the speaker considers true.

But it's also different from sarcasm. The term derives from the Greek *sarkasmós* (which refers to tearing, biting, tearing flesh) and the etymology helps to easily understand its intrinsic meaning. It is a form of bitter and pungent irony, inspired by animosity and therefore intended to offend and humiliate. Some linguistics experts consider it an "educated insult". The difference between irony and sarcasm is between what makes you smile and what hurts.

The borderline is thin, and the substantial differences can be recognized by the effect they produce. Irony has a beneficial, almost relaxing effect: it dissipates tensions, stimulates new thoughts and even if aimed at expressing

---

[80] Studies in evolutionary psychology have long found that understanding irony requires a complex interweaving of brain development, cognitive skills and socio-cognitive experiences. The development of the brain areas involved in this process matures in a long time and differs from person to person. The results of some of the first studies on the understanding of irony (in the 1980s) showed that at the age of 6, children are able to understand sincere communicative acts without any problems; the understanding of deception improved between the age of 6 and 13, and finally the understanding of irony started at the age of 13 (the data also showed that in adults irony was understood only in 50% of cases...).

disappointment, it is generally expressed with good intent. Irony implies creativity and, if carefully balanced, it is positive because it allows to get out of a hostile mood, relativizing the facts. Irony tends mainly to lighten the scenario and the comparison.

Instead, sarcasm seriously hurts. The aim of sarcasm is to sting, to make people feel guilty, to provoke negative reactions to achieve a personal goal, even if this is only to have psychological control over the other. Sarcasm is irony brought to excess with the aim of diminishing and degrading the other.

Sarcasm, therefore, involves primitive aggressive impulses, often unconscious, and is a tool of the weak who wants to appear strong and strike hard, making sure not to be attacked (because it was all part of a joke).

"Freedom begins with irony", said Victor Hugo. But using irony is not for everyone. Using irony is serious and should be used wisely. If it is badly constructed or misused, it can become very dangerous, especially in the legal field as it can produce effects exactly the opposite to the expectations.

To omit. *See* **To subtract**

2.13. To order

The order of the speech can be changed through specific rhetorical figures. The figures used can be distinguished in the figures (of speech) of permutation (which relates to an alteration of the usual order of the speech[81] by

---

[81] Some languages prefer the subject-predicate construction and therefore tends to place the theme (i.e. of which we speak) at

displacing the elements - e.g. anastrophe, hyperbaton and epiphrase) and in the figures (of thought) of order (which organize the topics of the speech in such a way as to modify its logical order).

2.13.1. Anastrophe[82] and hyperbaton[83]

Anastrophe is the inversion of the usual linear order of the enunciation (it is also called anteposition. Hyperbaton occurs when, among the elements of a statement connected syntactically, a segment of discourse /parenthetic is inserted.

The difference with the anastrophe is that while in the latter there is an inversion of two elements in the natural order of the words of a statement, in the hyperbaton one element wedges in another.

Some examples: "*Peace*, I need", "*Patience*, I lack"; similarly, in "This is the forest primeval", from Henry Wadsworth Longfellow's *Evangeline*, the emphasis is on 'primeval'; "Bloody thou art; bloody will be thy end" (William Shakespeare in *Richard III*, 4.4, 198); "Arms and the man I sing", opening words of Virgil's Aeneid etc.).

---

the beginning of the enunciation. The alteration of this order, as well as representing a contravention of a linguistic rule, has the effect of producing a change in the distribution of information and affecting the audience's (different) perception of it.

[82] From the Greek *anastrophé*, 'a turning back or about'; in Latin then *inversio*.

[83] From the Greek *hypérbaton* 'stepping over'.

2.13.2. *Epiphrase*[84]

It is a variant of the hyperbaton, and it involves adding an element (not necessary) to a statement, in such a position as to produce a hyperbaton between the added element and the elements is correlated to (e.g. "sweet and clear is the night, and without wind", Giacomo Leopardi).

It is mostly an elliptical and exclamative figure, as it comments on the content of the song that gets performed.

2.13.3. *Hysteron proteron*[85]

It is a figure of thought and relates to presenting a sequence of thoughts in reverse order to what would be natural from a logical or chronological point of view (e.g. "Acquittal, I ask. Because there is not even the objective element of the crime").

In terms of the content, it uses the same inversion mechanism in the syntactic field as the anastrophe[86].

2.14. To repeat

Repetition[87] relates to mentioning the same element in

---

[84] From the Greek *epiphrasis* 'added word'.

[85] From the Greek *hýsteron próteron* 'later earlier'.

[86] A typical example in journalism, however, is the relationship between 'title' and 'buttonhole' in the pages of newspapers, where one opts for an anticipation (also graphic, in this specific case) of a thought/element that should find an inverse place, because it appears more important or simply more suggestive than what has (logically or chronologically) determined or preceded it.

[87] The opposite of *repetition* (*repetitio*) is variation (*variatio*). The

different points of the statement, with two main aims: to facilitate the links between parts of text more or less distant from each other (favoring textual cohesion and understanding of the whole) and to enrich (embellish) a discourse. Only when used to achieve these aims, the repetitions are neither superfluous nor cumbersome.

However repetition in a speech (both written and oral) can concern several levels: phonetic and metric (rhymes, assonances, rhythmic cadences, alliterations), grammatical (with the use of the same syntactic structures), lexical (with the repetition of words), thematic (with the repetition of themes).

Repetition is considered a technique of 'presence', i.e. an instrument capable of presenting data in such a way to have a direct impact on the sensitivity of the audience.

The anaphora (or iteration), the epiphora, the epanalepsis and the anadiplosis are rhetorical figures of 'repetition' or accumulation, and mainly concern the lexical area: they impart 'images' that give to the words used expressive values which go beyond the current ones, generating in the interlocutor a sort of 'estrangement'.

2.14.1. *Anaphora*[88]

The anaphora is the figure of persistence, the model structure of repetition. It relates to the repetition of a word or group of words *at the beginning of* a sentence or verse (so-called textual segment), according to the

---

Latin rhetoricians recommended *variatio* as a remedy for unjustified stylistic repetitions (i.e. that they were not rhetorical figures).

[88] From the Greek *anaphorá* 'repetition ' (composed by *aná* 'again' and *phero* 'bring'); in Latin then *anaphora* and mainly *repetitio*.

following scheme[89]: "/x... /x.../". A classic example is Dante's: "*Through me* you pass into the city of woe; *through me* you pass into eternal pain; *through me* among the people lost for aye." (Dante, *Inferno*, III, 1-3).

A no less famous anaphora, however, is "*I have a dream*" (repeated 9 times) in the historic speech given by Martin Luther King Jr. on August 28, 1963 in front of the Lincoln Memorial in Washington at the end of the march for civil rights. It remains one of the most studied and cloned rhetorical examples.

But there are also many contemporary speakers who make use of anaphora. An example is Barack Obama, who often used the anaphora with ternary rhythm[90]: "*No* bailouts, *no* handouts, and *no* copouts" (Barack Obama, state of the union speech 2012); "This country has more wealth than any nation, *but that's not what* makes us rich. We have the most powerful military in history, *but that's not what* makes us strong. Our university, our culture are all the envy of the world, *but that's not what* keeps the world coming to our shores" (Barack Obama, re-election speech, 2012).

---

[89] Where the dots indicate the text segment, the *slash* (/) the interruption of the text segment and the 'x' the word/group of words being repeated.

[90] The ternary rhythm is the repetition of three elements. From a rhythmic point of view, accumulations with more than three members can be weaker by excess, while binary structures (accumulations with only two members) can be weaker by default. The ternary ones instead seem the most 'harmonic': in the number three, in fact, there is a center and there are two extremes, while in the numbers two and four there is no center on which the attention can be focused on so that each part seems to be linked to it.

2.14.2. Polysyndeton[91]

It is a particular form of anaphoric repetition that relates to coordinating several syntactic elements (single words, sentences) by a systematically repeated conjunction (e.g. "The defendant gets out *and* takes the car *and* runs fast *and* arrives inexorably at the victim's home"; similarly in literature: "I said, 'Who killed him?' *and* he said 'I don't know who killed him, but he's dead all right,' *and* it was dark *and* there was water standing in the street *and* no lights or windows broke *and* boats all up in the town *and* trees blown down and everything all blown *and* I got a skiff *and* went out *and* found my boat where I had her inside Mango Key *and* she was right only she was full of water" - Ernest Hemingway, *After the Storm*).

2.14.3. Epiphora[92] or epistrophe[93]

It mirrors the anaphora and relates to the repetition of a word or group of words *at the end of* a textual segment, according to the scheme: "/...x/...x/" (e.g. "The defendant went out *drunk*, came home *drunk*, woke up *drunk*"; "[...] this nation, under God, shall have a new birth of freedom - and that government *of the people, by the people, for the people*, shall not perish from the earth", Abraham Lincoln in the *Gettysburg Address*).

Like the anaphora, it characterizes different types of discourse that use (albeit with different communicative purposes) parallelisms. In the oratory technique, it is

---

[91] From the Greek *polý* 'many' and *syndèo* 'put together'.

[92] From the Greek *epiphorá* 'addition, conclusion' (therefore, 'bring in addition').

[93] From the Greek *epistrophé* 'return'.

generally used to raise the register of the dictation and to capture the attention.

2.14.4. Symploce[94]

It is the combination of anaphora and epiphora, where the beginning and the end of a statement of any length can become the beginning or the end of one or more successive statements according to the different scheme: "/x...y/x...y/" (e.g. "Beware of envious man, always; beware of envying man, always").

A splendid example of combined use of epiphora and anaphora, in ternary rhythm, can be found in the last sentence of the speech made by Queen Elizabeth on April 5, 2020 during the pandemic: "*We will* be with our friends *again*, *we will* be with our families *again*; *we will* meet *again*" (note the repetition of '*we will*' as an anaphora, and '*again*' as an epiphora, both repeated three times).

2.14.5. Polyptoton[95]

In this figure of repetition a word is repeated in the same statement (or in contiguous and connected statements) with different syntactic functions (e.g. "hand in hand"; "Not as a call to battle, though embattled we are", John F. Kennedy, Inaugural Address, January 20, 1961).

In general, it characterizes many idiomatic expressions. Combining two opposite rhetorical mechanisms (repetition and variation), it is often used to achieve other figures of repetition (epanalepsis, anadiplosis, anaphora)

---

[94] From the Greek *symploké* 'plot'.
[95] From the Greek *polýptoton* 'of many cases'.

precisely to mitigate the repetition itself.

2.14.6. *Epanalepsis*[96]

It relates to the consecutive repetition (doubling) of a word or group of words at the beginning of a textual segment (pattern: "/aa.../" - e.g. "I know, I know; people will think I keep repeating the same things") or within it (pattern: "/...aa.../" - e.g. "Of course - I know, I know – people will think that I keep repeating the same things").

It is a rather common type of figure (also in the variant with possible advertisements among 'clones' - e.g. "Careful, guys, careful").

Like the other figures of repetition, epanalepsis aims to highlight already formulated concepts that, through iteration, can attract attention and impress more easily on the memory of the audience.

2.14.7. *Epizeuxis*[97]

The addition of further repetitions of the word or group of words to an epanalepsis leads to another rhetorical figure called epizeuxis, which relates to multiple repetitions with iconic effect (e.g. "And walk, walk, walk").

---

[96] From the Greek *epanálepsys* 'resumption, repetition, taking up again' (composed of *pálin* 'again' and *légo* 'say').
[97] From the Greek *epízeuxis* 'union'.

2.14.8. *Anadiplosis*[98]

It relates to the repetition of the last word(s) of a statement at the beginning of the next one, according to the scheme: "...x/x..." (e.g. "In the end what is missing is the *motive*, the *motive that* seemed so obvious").

The repeated word can also be represented by a synonym (e.g. "In the end what is missing is the *motive*, the reason *why killing him that* seemed so obvious"; "What I present here is what I remember of the letter, and what I remember of the letter I remember verbatim (including that awful French)", Vladimir Nabokov, *Lolita*): in this way, not only does it lighten the speech but it provides it with more information and intensifies it.

The longer the interposition, the more this figure becomes necessary to avoid possible ambiguities of meaning and to make it clear to which element the following statements should refer. It is therefore one of the most frequent rhetorical figures, in every type of discourse, from the least to the most formal, especially (and necessarily) in the most complex elaborations.

However, the more the contact between repeated words loosens, the more indecisive the line between anadiplosis and anaphora will appear.

The effects achieved by this figure are however multiple: from thematic and rhythmic reinforcement to evocative suggestion.

---

[98] From the Greek *anadíplosis* 'a doubling, folding up' - in Latin then *reduplicatio*.

2.14.9. Climax[99]

It is that rhetorical figure of speech, also called gradation or ascending gradation, which relates to gradually moving from one concept to another, or repeating a unique concept with increasingly effective and intense synonymous words, or more generically arranging the terms of a sentence in an increasing order of value and strength (e.g. "I will limit myself to show you how in this trial something, the fact, the crime, has been missing: everything!"; also in literature: "Lost, vaded, broken, dead within an hour", William Shakespeare, *The Passionate Pilgrim*, XIII).

The oldest scheme of the *climax* is that of a continuous anadiplosis ("...x/x...y/y...z/z..."), proceeding precisely by 'steps', stopping on each one before moving to the next; and each 'step' on which one stops becomes the first of the next.

In order to increase the intensity and give emphasis to a speech, one writes and speaks as one climbs up the stairs. The *climax* (a word that truly means 'ladder') works like this: for each word, for each expression, you give a little more strength to the speech, you choose words that are more and more intense, as it happens when you go up a ladder and each step is a little higher, you bring a little more emphasis than the previous one. The emotion of the reader or listener grows with the words: after every comma, there is something stronger waiting for him.

But you can also go down the stairs. In fact, descending is sometimes the only thing to do when you have

---

[99] The term is a Grecism of Latin and Italian (in Greek *klímax* 'staircase'); another term used is the Latin *gradatio*. The original Greek and Latin term (in both cases feminine) becomes with masculine; the feminine form remains instead relegated to specialist rhetorical use.

reached the top, especially in contexts where it is then appropriate to lighten the tone. So there is also the opposite of the *climax*, the decline of the emphasis, the deflation: this is called the *anticlimax*. Here too we work on the intensity of the speech, but in the opposite direction: we aim to remove, to soften. And then it gradually degrades towards a lower intensity (e.g. "She no longer had the strength to fight it and remained there still, silent, immobile").

2.14.10. *Alliteration*[100]

The repetition can also be a repetition of sounds[101]. Alliteration is precisely the resort to identical vowels, consonants, and syllables at the beginning of two or more consecutive words, or even within them.

The alliteration obtained with initial sounds is phonically what the anaphora is syntactically and lexically. But, like any figure of repetition, alliteration can also become annoying when it adds nothing to the consistency of the level (lexical, syntactic, phonic, rhythmic), remaining a useless exercise of style.

---

[100] From Latin *allitteratio*, neologism coined in the fifteenth century by the humanist Giovanni Pontano.

[101] In general, homophony plays an important role in the process of 'memorizing' a statement. In fact, the use of these patterns and figures is recurrent in all those kinds of speech in which 'memorability' is an essential part of the communication strategies (e.g. advertising slogans).

2.14.11. *Homeoteleuton*[102]

Also spelled homoeoteleuton and homoioteleuton, it is a figure mirroring alliteration and relates to the phonic equality of the ending of words adjacent or close to each other (e.g. "a man with false *teeth* and great *disbelief*").

2.15. To sentence

2.15.1. *Sententia*

In rhetoric, *sententia* is a universal statement, formulated in a short and concise style, the content of which is generally accepted, applicable to a multitude of different but similar cases.

Although consistent with the discourse, this figure is (as far as the meaning is concerned) a complete discourse in itself, a consequent condensation of an idea, a short discourse in the discourse, with well-defined formal and content aspects, and self-sufficiency (e.g. "All that is excellent is rare").

But *sententia* is a generic term for several specific varieties: the maxim, the aphorism, the proverb.

2.15.2. *Maxim*

It relates to the major premise of the *sententia*, i.e. it is the assumption that it does not require further argumentative evidence and is, therefore, less bound to the parts of the speech that possibly precede it (e.g. "*dura lex, sed lex*").

---

[102] From the Greek *homoiotéleuton* 'like ending'.

2.15.3. Aphorism[103]

It is a sentence characterized by defining skills and, although currently considered linguistically equivalent to the maxim, it differs from it because of its different formal articulation. While the maxim derives its effectiveness from tradition and therefore does not require any evidence, the aphorism - although characterized by brevity and conciseness - tends instead to subvert common opinions through the use of paradox and irony (e.g. "Many judges are incorruptible, nothing can induce them to do justice", Bertold Brecht).

2.15.4. Proverb

It condenses in a sentence, characterized by brevity and conciseness, a moral precept dictated by common sense or a rule of life drawn from experience.

To imply *See* To subtract

2.16. To subtract

Subtracting, but also omitting, implying, deleting: we will examine rhetorical figures characterized by the subtraction of elements of speech, and therefore defined as figures of thought by subtraction or deduction.

The deduction is the procedure that relates to omitting elements that would be necessary for the syntactical

---

[103] From the Greek *aphorismós* 'delimitation, distinction, definition'; then in Latin *aphorismus*.

or thematic completeness of a statement.

The figures by deduction are used for the realization of a *brevis* style, because they also avoid unnecessary repetitions. But they are also capable of triggering in the audience or the readers a wait-and-see mechanism, which will dissolve only when it is possible to integrate the intentionally missing information. This causes the typical alienating effect of rhetorical figures.

2.16.1. Brachyology, conciseness or brevitas

The term brachyology is not intended to indicate a specific figure, but rather a stylistic ideal[104] that can be achieved through different figures both in terms of content and means of expression, using schemes such as laconism[105] and figures such as *percursio*, preterition and reticence.

2.16.2. Percursio[106]

It relates to a brief enumeration of thematic motifs (which would need to be treated analytically) with a broad and detailed presentation of each of them. A sort of 'summary' without 'details': a quick and essential review of

---

[104] "We achieve brevity not by saying less but by not saying more than is necessary (...) by saying what is necessary and enough (...) brevity must not be unadorned, in which case it would be crude": Quint., *Inst. orat.*, IV, 2, 43.

[105] A model of conciseness, for the ancients, was the way of speaking of the Spartans. Hence the term 'laconism', which became in Latin "*Laconica brevitas*", which means to reduce a speech to the essential but characterized by incisive effectiveness.

[106] From the Latin *percurro* 'run through'.

facts and events, a story reduced to the essential, a brilliant and incisive synthesis[107].

2.16.3. Ellipse[108]

It is a rhetorical expedient to simplify a speech (mainly written speech) by eliminating repetition. It can be considered the model-figure of detraction.

The syntactical omission that the ellipsis entails can lead to greater incisiveness of speech, but it can also generate semantic obscurity, leaving the overall meaning of the enunciation indefinite. It will then be up to the addressee, also in this case, to reconstruct it or (with a decidedly alienating effect) wait for it to be clarified by the continuation of the discourse (so-called cataphoric ellipsis).

2.16.4. Preterition[109]

It relates to affirming that one wants to pass over something in silence at the very moment in which it is mentioned, thus giving it greater emphasis.

---

[107] The typical classical example is Caesar's *"veni, vidi, vici"* ("I came, I saw, I won").

[108] From the Latin *ellipsis*, transcription of the Greek *élleipsis* ('omission').

[109] From the Latin *praeteritio* 'omission' (from *praetereo* 'I go beyond'). The Latin rhetoric considered it a remedy for any flaws by default with respect to the criteria of *brevitas* and *aptum*. However, the figure represented a formal safe-conduct and made it possible to say the unspeakable, that is, what could not be enunciated either because it was rough or because it was marginal with respect to the main argument of the discourse.

It is rather widespread also in everyday language (e.g. "not to mention", "better not say that") and also in more formal contexts ("leaving aside any comment on his numerous criminal records"). It has a meta-communicative informative content: it attracts attention and makes the audience think about the unsaid. It is the emphasis on the unspoken[110].

However, the correct use of this figure implies (like irony and other rhetorical figures), between speaker and audience, a shared knowledge of which the omitted information would be part (also called common ground). When such shared knowledge is missing, the figure would not be possible or could represent an even more deleterious illation (especially in a particularly technical and formal context)[111].

2.16.5. *Aposiopesis*[112] *or reticence*

It relates to the sudden interruption of a message by suppressing a part of it or the direct allusion to something that is kept quiet (e.g. "He was a guy who calls himself quiet, but…").

---

[110] The paradoxically emphatic character of this figure is well outlined in the *Rhetorica ad Herennium* as relating to "saying that we do not know or do not want to say what we say most effectively at that very moment" (*Rhet. Ad Her.*, IV, 27).

[111] Illation (from the Latin *illatio* and *illatus*, and these from *inferre* 'to carry') relates to a judgment formulated deductively which, however, results in an arbitrary hypothesis (conjecture or supposition).

[112] From the Greek *aposiópesis* (from *asiopáo*, 'becoming silent'), then in Latin *reticentia*. In ancient rhetoric it was considered one of the possible forms of thematic transition or *transitio*, i.e. used by the speaker to change the subject.

Through self-censorship, reticence emphasizes the value of the 'unspoken', and what is implicit conveys a greater informative content and also a semantic value compared to what is explicitly said. It is not by chance that we speak of "rhetoric of silence".

The reticence relies heavily on the interpretation of the recipient, whose role becomes more active as the speech becomes more discreet. This can also consist of prosodic means (the suspended intonation for oral texts and the suspension dots - three - for written ones) and kinesics signals (glance and aversion, facial expressions etc.).

The allusive power of silence then makes reticence an extremely effective instrument to convey insinuation, suspicion, or threat.

2.16.6. *Asyndeton*[113]

It is the ellipse of the conjunction between words and phrases, syntactically linked (e.g. "he looked out the window, saw a shadow, became frightened, fired into the dark"; "and that government of the people, by the people, for the people shall not perish from the earth", Abraham Lincoln, *Gettysburg Address*). It is coordination without a conjunction (and, therefore, the opposite of polysyndeton).

It is used to create an *abruptus* style (broken, interrupted[114]), with a hammering effect, and is particularly suitable for the motion of affections, giving emphasis and in general greater effectiveness to the enunciation.

---

[113] From the Greek *asýndeton* 'unconnected'.
[114] From the Latin *abrumpo* 'I break'.

2.17. To explain

Sometimes the speaker needs to clarify issues or individual statements without being repetitive.

There are rhetorical figures (of thought by addition) aimed precisely at thematic amplification and semantic clarification, where the objective is to make the speaker's argument more explicit and understandable and to give it emotional extent or intensity.

2.17.1. Commoratio[115]

It relates to the persistent repetition of the same thoughts, using different words to achieve an effect of amplification or semantic intensification. Repetition can be aimed at clarifying a concept in all its nuances or at clarifying or highlighting only certain aspects of it.

It can come in two forms: *expolitio* and *interpretatio*.

2.17.2. Expolitio[116]

This is a form of *commoratio* which relates to returning to the same theme by adding complementary information and changing the expression so that it becomes more energetic in the consciousness and memory of the audience (e.g. "Can we still talk about the effectiveness of the doubtful formula? Can we still believe that this formula is worth something?")[117].

---

[115] From the Latin *morari* 'to linger'.

[116] From the Latin *expólio* 'I perfect'.

[117] A classic example is the *incipit* of Cicero's first speech against Catiline: "How long will you abuse, Oh Catiline, our

2.17.3. Interpretatio

This is another form of *commoratio* which is also called interpretative paraphrase and relates to putting another equivalent to a statement, to clarify and enrich the thoughts already expressed (e.g. "Can we still talk about the effectiveness of the doubtful formula? Can we still have the certainty that the doubt is correctly evaluated by the judges and leads to acquittal?"). The interpretative paraphrase is similar, as far as the results are concerned, to the definition.

2.17.4. Definition[118]

It relates to explicitly stating the meaning of a word. It is a synthetic statement; it serves to present the essence of the concept. It is the ultimate result of the dialectical division. It is also used to highlight certain aspects that might risk remaining obscure or to underline a meaning that is favorable to one's opinion (e.g. "Rhetoric is the art of persuasive discourse: it means 'practice' and 'theory', i.e. eloquence and system of norms to be followed to be 'eloquent').

One form of definition is etymology, which relates to the explanation of the meaning of a word starting from its etymology, i.e. its original meaning (e.g. "Sarcasm - the Greek etymology itself tells us - is a form of bitter and pungent irony, inspired by animosity").

---

patience? How much longer will this madness of yours mock us? How far will this unbridled insolence of yours go?"

[118] In Latin *finitio* 'define the boundaries, delimit'.

2.17.5. *Epanorthosis*[119] *or correctio*

It relates to the substitution (explicit and declared) of the word just used with another one more appropriate to the context (usually a word with a similar but more intense and effective meaning - e.g. "He approached him and spoke to him, or rather shouted at him"), with different corrective formulas ("not x, but y"; y, not x"; x, or rather y"; "x, but what do I say x? y!"; "Thousands, no, millions!").

Obviously, the function is rhetoric, and nothing to do with involuntary *lapsus*[120] correction.

---

[119] In Greek *epanórthosis* 'correcting, revision'.

[120] Used to indicate the error resulting from a substitution, transposition or involuntary omission of a word in writing (*lapsus calami*) or speaking (*lapsus linguae*).

3. Argumentative fallacies

3.1. Introduction and definition

In reasoning, a fallacy produces the same effect as a false visual perception: it seems to work but, if you analyze it better, it hides reasoning that is only apparently correct.

After all, in a false visual perception (or even 'optical illusion') we are led to recognize figures that in reality do not exist or differ in particular characteristics, usually not visible except after careful observation. This happens because the human brain is attracted by some elements that are more common and known to it, or because it is deceived or disturbed in identifying the true nature of an image from the details.

These phenomena are precisely called optical illusions and are designed to capture the observer's attention.

For example, let's look at this figure:

Do the horizontal lines appear converging and crooked? They are perfectly parallel.

The aim of the fallacies is precisely to simulate logically correct reasoning which, on closer examination, 'does not work'.

Fallacies are incorrect ways of reasoning because either one starts from false premises, or one adopts incorrect inferences, or one produces, in support of one's theses, arguments that are irrelevant from a rational point of view.

Therefore, it is important to distinguish an enthymeme from a fallacy: when in an enthymeme the premises are false, only then we speak of fallacy. The enthymeme does not represent always a 'fallacy', but only when the premise omitted is false. The enthymeme (unlike the fallacy) has nothing to do with imperfection but with the implicit, to become faster, more pleasant, allusive, curious.

This does not stop the use of fallacies: one does not always want to rely on the rationality of the interlocutor, and sometimes it is easier to focus on emotions or it is more effective to resort to deception. Fallacies are used in diverse contexts, precisely because of the difficulty of being recognized as such: their apparent correctness makes them particularly suitable to intentionally and fraudulently manipulate the audience, to produce a deceptive persuasion (e.g. fake news).

Fallacies are therefore logical errors that arise from (often intentional) flaws which are used to build the arguments of public discourse in every area: social networks, politics, advertising, journalism, storytelling. Indeed, a large part of modern communication is affected by these 'flaws', including procedural communication.

The term 'fallacy' therefore seems to have almost naturally a negative meaning, because fallacies are particular 'errors' of reasoning and are considered 'hidden persuaders'.

It is argued that accurate and strategic use of argumentative fallacies can sometimes make the discourse more persuasive and effective than completely logical reasoning; and, therefore, transform 'vice' into 'virtue'. However, there are considerable perplexities (logical, ethical, and deontological) around the acceptance (even partial) of such an approach in the legal field. In legal discourse, argumentative fallacies can certainly be an unconscious expression of a logical vice (dictated by inexperience), but also a conscious expression of stratagems aimed at supporting unfounded theses. In both cases they are used with serious damages to the legal system as a whole, to the profession, and to the quality of the law itself: in democratic systems, the judicial process forces the parties and the judge to be heard, which must be characterized by rules of argumentation that are effectively respected. And fallacies are violations of such rules.

The goal of the lawyers must be a rationally persuasive argument, not persuasion by seduction.

3.2. A good argument

If fallacies are errors of reasoning, we should ask ourselves what reasoning (that is, arguing) really means and highlight some elements that will allow us to recognize fallacies more easily.

A topic (the subject of the argument) is made up of a series of premises that rationally support a certain conclusion. To 'argue' then means to 'fit together' statements in an appropriate way, so that some of them (the premises) are in support of another statement (the conclusion).

However premises and conclusion do not always find

their natural place, since the conclusion (for example) can be placed at the beginning of the statement (e.g. "He cannot sustain the final discussion; he has not yet passed the last exam": in this argument, developed in the form of an explanation of the conclusion, the premise is reported after the conclusion).

It should also be noted that there are conversational subtexts, which are particularly relevant in the formulation of rhetorical questions and certain types of fallacies (e.g. "You have already wasted enough time on this issue. It is, therefore, time to move on to something else", this represents a topic developed with structural regularity, but can also be rendered in the form of a rhetorical question: "Haven't you already wasted enough time on this issue?").

When can an argument then be defined, from a logical point of view, a 'good argument'? When: a) its premises are plausible; b) they are relevant to the conclusion; c) given these premises, it is very likely (though not certain) that the conclusion will follow.

Conversely, fallacies represent errors of the argument in which a reasoning, although not logically correct, is somehow convincing and persuasive (on a strictly communicative level).

However paradoxical that might seem (and not acceptable in many contexts), some logical-argumentative errors, if used properly, can make the argument more persuasive than perfectly correct reasoning from a logical-argumentative point of view.

(cont'd) Classification of fallacies

The types of fallacies are countless. Aristotle was the first to classify fallacies. He identified thirteen logical fallacies, distributed in two different categories: linguistic and non-linguistic fallacies. Since then, the evolution of the different argumentative techniques and the evolution of the language have led to new argumentative fallacies.

It can be safely argued that there are no universal criteria for classifying them. There are classification schemes that are very similar in number and type of items, however, they classify the same argumentation scheme differently or group the argumentation schemes in different ways.

There is, however, some agreement on 'what' the fallacies are. There are about twenty fallacies that appear in almost all theories.

A particularly well-known classification (which may be relevant here) is the distinction between:
-   semantic fallacies: they derive from the vague or ambiguous use of terms and linguistic expressions;
-   formal fallacies: they result from the use of invalid or valid but misapplied rules of inference;
-   inductive fallacies: they derive from inferring a conclusion that has a lower inductive probability than it is assumed;
-   fallacies of presumption: when the truth of what is intended to be proven is presumed;
-   fallacies of relevance: these occur when the premises have a little relevance to the conclusion.

We will examine only some of the fallacies that may be relevant and useful in the forensic field[121].

-----

[121] Moreover, it is a subject - fallacies - which is studied mainly in logic, philosophy of law and philosophy of science.

3.3. Semantic fallacies

They derive from the vague or ambiguous use of terms and linguistic expressions (it should be noted that ambiguity and vagueness are only apparently interchangeable terms).

Starting from the concept of ambiguity[122], we distinguish between lexical ambiguity and structural (or syntactic) ambiguity.

3.3.1. Lexical ambiguity. Fallacy of the fourth term

A statement is lexically ambiguous when it contains a term, or more than one, with multiple meanings. For example, ambiguous words like 'bats'. The sentence "I saw *bats*" could be interpreted in four different ways: 'I used a tool with a sharp blade to slice through baseball bats'; 'I viewed some nocturnal flying mammals'; 'I viewed baseball bats'; 'I used a tool with a sharp blade to slice through nocturnal flying mammals'. Viewed without the context of adjacent sentences, this sentence is easily misinterpreted. Here's another example: "Insurance salesmen are frightening people". It is not possible to determine exactly what this sentence is attempting to convey: are insurance salesmen scaring people into buying their insurance, or are the salesmen themselves scary?

A typical fallacy of lexical ambiguity is the fallacy of the fourth term: it derives its name from Aristotelian syllogism (only three terms must be used: the major premise, the minor premise, and the conclusion) and occurs when an erroneous conclusion is dealt with precisely

---

[122] From the Latin *ambíguitas*, composed of *amb* 'both' and *agere* 'to drive': metaphorically, 'to drive on one side and on the other'.

because an ambiguous term is interpreted with two different meanings in the premises of the same argument - and for this reason, it is called 'fourth term' (although only three terms are used).

3.3.2. *Structural ambiguity. Amphiboly*[123]. *Fallacy of accent*

A sentence is structurally ambiguous when the terms it contains have a single meaning, but their arrangement in the sentence allows for multiple interpretations.

The fallacy called amphiboly is when, within the same argument, two or more different meanings are attributed to the same structurally ambiguous sentence, thus drawing an incorrect conclusion[124] (e.g. "One morning I shot an elephant in my pajamas"; "We took some pictures of the native girls, but they weren't developed. But we're going back again in a couple of weeks" - from *Animal Crackers*, 1930, a Marx brothers movie).

Another form of structural ambiguity is the one that forms the basis of another fallacy frequently used, the fallacy of the accent. It occurs when, within the same subject, it is possible to place the focus (i.e. the importance) on more than one element of the same statement, with consequent and different interpretations.

---

[123] From the Greek *amphíbolia* 'double meaning' (from *amphí* '*on* one side and the other' and *bállo* 'I throw').

[124] It is typical of the oracular language (in antiquity) and of some daily headlines ("Farmer kills himself after a farewell to his family with a rifle shot"). These are expressions that have at least two meanings and from time to time the context or the intonation will indicate (or leverage) which of the meanings is appropriate.

3.3.3. *Vagueness. The paradox of Sorites*[125]

A term is said to be vague when, although it has a precise meaning and cannot be confused with different meanings, it is nevertheless difficult to identify exactly the boundaries within which it can be properly used (e.g. rich/poor, high/low, big/small etc.).

The paradox of Sorites is precisely a paradox that is characterized by some vague predicates, i.e. predicates for which there is no clear dividing line between their scope and their non-application.

However, there are also vague predicates that do not lead to paradoxes of fate: for example, non-dimensional evaluative predicates such as 'beautiful', 'intelligent'.

3.4. Emotional fallacies

These are fallacies based on *pathos*, rather than *logos*.

3.4.1. *Argumentum ad baculum*[126] *(appeal to force)*

It occurs when, instead of supporting a conclusion based on the plausibility of the premises, one is invited to draw

---

[125] In the etymological sense it means 'heap' and is originally a sophisticated argument attributed to Eubulid of Miletus and widely used by Greek skeptics to demonstrate the impossibility of distinguishing true from false. The most common way in which it was formulated was as follows: the first grain does not constitute a pile, the second does not constitute a pile etc.; either the pile is never constituted or, if it is admitted that it is constituted by the addition of a given grain, one must conclude that it was that one grain that made the pile be.

[126] From the Latin, 'stick'.

that conclusion based on an appeal to force and intimidation (e.g. an inconvenient witness is vindicated for slander).

3.4.2. *Argumentum ad metum*[127] *(appeal to fear)*

It relates to inducing fear of the consequences that the acceptance of the opposing argument would cause (e.g. "the non-acceptance of this proposal would undoubtedly provoke a reaction of the whole office, which would manifest itself very soon").

3.4.3. *Argumentum ad misericordiam (appeal to pity)*

It relates to trying to trigger compassion in the audience by using reasons clearly in contrast with the facts (famous is the example of the parricide whose defender concludes "at least have pity on a poor orphan!").

3.4.4. *Argumentum ad hominem*

It relates to discrediting the opposing party by questioning its credibility, competence, impartiality etc.

It can be of two types: prevaricating (when attacking the character of the opponent) and circumstantial (when the attack is based on the circumstances of the opponent or the role he plays, which would not allow him to support a certain thesis).

---

[127] From the Latin *metus* 'fear' (therefore, 'appeal to fear').

3.4.5. Poisoning the Well

It is a form of *ad hominem* circumstantial fallacy and relates to a preventive attack to undermine in advance the credibility of everything, according to the following argumentative scheme: 1) A is unreliable; 2) everything A claims is false or otherwise unacceptable (e.g. "My reconstruction of what happened is the pure truth. I am sure that Mr. Johnson will tell the exact opposite, but Mr. Johnson has serious problems of alcoholism and relational difficulties")[128].

It may be supported by allegations of prejudice, interest, or incompetence against the opponent.

3.4.6. *Argumentum ad populum (appeal to common belief)*

One argues about the truth or falsity of a statement by appealing to popular sentiment. However, the positive (or negative) emotional value of an event, object, or person does not imply a similar value of truth (positive or negative: i.e. true or false) for the statements that refer to it.

---

[128] The name derives from the ancient practice of poisoning one's own wells to stop invasions by enemy armies and is taken as an emblematic example of a technique as simple to perform as it is devastating in its effects.

3.5. Other relevant fallacies

3.5.1. *Argumentum ad verecundiam*[129] *(appeal to authority)*

It is the argument of authority (or even an appeal to authority), which relates to trying to escape the duty of proof, presenting one's statements as self-evident, guaranteeing their correctness personally or because they are sponsored by an expert.

Consequently, it is a dogmatic appeal to the authority to censure as insolent, anyone who opposes the authority, exposing them to blame and reprobation.

The fallacious use of this argument would occur when the authority is used to force critical discussion to an early closure.

3.5.2. *Argumentum ad ignorantiam (appeal to ignorance)*

This form of argument is used whenever it is inferred that a proposition is true simply because it has not been proven to be false, or that it is false because it has not been proven to be true.

This is an obvious stratagem, aimed at reversing the duty of proof and of an appropriate argument.

There is, however, one case, in the legal field, where its use is legitimate: the presumption of innocence of the accused until his guilt is proven beyond reasonable doubt and recognized by a final judgment.

---

[129] From the Latin *verecundia* 'feeling shame'.

3.5.3. Red herring (irrelevant conclusion)

The fallacy occurs when an attempt is made to present an argument where the premises have nothing to do with the conclusion (e.g. when, to influence the jury against a defendant, the prosecutor focuses on the consideration that the crime is a horrible thing and that the type of crime of which the defendant is accused is particularly horrible).

It is a technique of escaping from an uncomfortable subject, putting another subject out of the question.

This logical fallacy is often used in an intentional attempt to confuse or distract the interlocutor. The expression 'red herring' derives from the custom of salting and smoking herrings (which as a consequence becomes reddish-brownish) to preserve them for a long time. During fox hunting campaigns the smoked herrings distracted the dogs from the track and could be used by hunters to divert the dogs of competing hunters from the track.

In literature and cinema, the 'red herring' is a narrative tactic aimed at directing the reader/spectator towards a wrong conclusion.

3.5.4. Straw man fallacy

The straw man fallacy allows to elaborate an unfaithful representation of the opponentto tear it down. The straw man is an excessive and caricatured reworking of the opponent's thesis to facilitate its refutation. The realization of the 'straw man' takes place by plausibly exaggerating the adversary's thesis and then demolishing it.

This fallacy does not address the subject in question, it is a kind of red herring fallacy. Its function is to awaken, based on how easily it can be demolished, a feeling of derision or disapproval that can be addressed to the real figure that represents it.

3.5.5. *Plurium interrogationum (complex question)*

It relates to asking a question in such a way as to presuppose the truth of a conclusion (e.g. "Are you still using drugs?"). The answer with a "yes" or "no" is simplistic, since the question is indeed 'complex' and presupposes (at least) another question.

The aim is usually to catch unprepared the interlocutor, often exploiting particularly delicate contexts from a psychological point of view. For example, it is also used as a trivial interrogation technique: a question is asked that implies the existence of a fact or a supposed truth ("After you killed him, where did you hide the corpse?"). The questioned person, however, he answers (with a yes or a no), inevitably admits the unexplained assumption ("How am I to get in?" asked Alice again, in a louder tone. "Are you to get in at all?" said the Footman, "That's the first question, you know" - Lewis Carroll, *Alice's Adventures in Wonderland*).

3.5.6. *Argumentum ad consequentiam (appeal to consequences of a belief)*

It is an argument that concludes a hypothesis (typically a belief) to be either true or false based on whether the premise leads to desirable or undesirable consequences.

This kind of argument is fallacious because the premises only concern the consequences that seem likely to arise from the acceptance of the conclusion, and not its truth (e.g. one devalues a testimony given by a psychically unstable or immature person, on the assumption that such a person is unreliable).

A particular type of *argumentum ad consequentiam* is the so-called 'slippery slope' which consists of arguing against the decision to take a certain course of action because of the devastating consequences that could result, without proving or supporting the consequential link with sufficient evidence.

3.5.7. *Petitio principii (circular logic)*

This is achieved when the conclusion is taken as a premise. The classic theoretical example is in itself funny: a bank asks Mr. Johnson to name a person who will vouch for him; Mr. Johnson names his friend Mr. Black and when asked "How do we know he is a reliable person?", Mr. Johnson answers: "He is: I assure you".

3.5.8. *Secundum quid (hasty generalization)*

It relates to deriving a general rule from insufficient evidence, either because it links to a special case, or because the sample considered is not representative (e.g. "Since drug use is allowed for the seriously ill, it should be allowed for anyone").

3.5.9. *False precision (over precision or fake precision)*

This fallacy is achieved when extremely precise numbers are cited, to induce the audience to believe that the information presented is trustworthy. The numbers are used to make people believe that the content of their statement is perfectly reliable, taken from official sources.

The fallacy of false precision never fails to awaken a kind of explanatory and self-referential evidence, often exempting the speaker from enlightening data and numbers, as if they were immediately clear and persuasive.

4. Visual rhetoric

4.1. The visual - support and topic

The Roman lawyer (*orator*) recognized the importance of the suggestion of images and was able to translate it into words, whereas today the contemporary lawyer mainly uses images as a mere support or pure instrument of suggestion as to absorb words and the image is used to synthesize and fascinate. If Quintilian emphasized the need for an audience capable of receiving and in turn re-elaborating the 'words' into images, today we could argue that the speaker is aware that he is faced with an audience capable of understanding an image more easily and more quickly than a description made of words.

Although the modern speaker is confronted with subjects formed in an era strongly conditioned by the overwhelming power of visuals and speed, he is technically incapable - because he is no longer trained[130] - of the full and correct use of speech and rhetoric. The use of the visual is therefore natural and practical. Also, concerning the use of the visuals, there is certainly no awareness by the jurists of its argumentative value, being almost

---

[130] The *deficit* is not only European but is also detected overseas (Sherwin 2018).

relegated to the role of mere support.

The ancient rhetoricians succeeded in making words stronger than images. Through the *evidentia*, they showed us how verbal communication can match the persuasive power of images. As long as there is also a reader/listener who is attentive to *concipere imagines*[131].

Therefore, with Quintilian the idea of the ability, even though minimal, of the reader/listener to perceive the *evidentia* emerges clearly: the vivid representation is not something that is readily-given to the reader, but it is a text that requires collaboration precisely in terms of imagination[132].

Imagination is the mechanism to visualize the text. It is a mental mechanism of vivid representation so that one can see images of facts and scenes that he is not seeing in person, so that he has the impression of having them in front of his eyes.

It must therefore be the speaker (in particular, the lawyer) who does not use a painting but elaborates the images already in his mind. From the elaborated text/discourse the impression of direct vision and expressive immediacy arises, which the rhetorical tradition identifies with the quality of *enárgeia*.

In Quintilian the mechanism of fantastic imagination is central in the process of evoking *páthos* and, consequently, *phantasía* and *evidentia* become central in the persuasion of the audience.

---

[131] Quintilian cites the description of Verres dashed by Cicero in the *Pro Gallium*, unfortunately lost: Quint., *Inst. orat.*, VIII, 64.

[132] Already Demetrius (*eloc.* 222) and Dionysius (*Lys.*, 7, 2 Aujac) stress that the descriptive precision in which the evidence consists does not mean to say everything but to let the reader/listener add the unexpressed details through his imagination, in order to involve him more directly. There is a risk, in fact, that excessive descriptivism will cool the *páthos* of the scene.

Therefore, Quintilian and his predecessors seem to have found a solution that preserves the word from the overwhelming power of images, leaving its communicative effectiveness unchanged: it is the word that makes itself image.

However, the speaker must be capable of imagining and an interlocutor willing to do so[133].

Today, in times when images are often overpowering tools of speech, some scholars (towards the end of the last century, starting with Barthes in 1964) have begun to question whether images could then have an autonomous capacity to 'argue' (thus diverting the study of argumentation, traditionally linked to the dimension of verbal language alone).

However, since early studies of visual argumentation, there has been resistance to the idea that images can be 'arguments'. In general, the attitude of most scholars has been that argumentation is closely related to the explicit use of words[134].

It has been argued that the argument can be accompanied by the use of non-verbal media, but without the use of language it cannot be considered an 'argument'. There is more: since we cannot distinguish between premise and conclusion in an image, and since images cannot provide statements that can be contested (since an image only shows something), images cannot be 'arguments' by definition[135].

---

[133] Basically, Quintilian identifies the *evidentia* as the first quality of literary illusion.

[134] Which is not surprising, since the study of argumentation has been a study of verbal communication for over 2,000 years.

[135] According to this approach, the only role that a painting could play, for example, is as a support for verbal premises, and this is only possible if visual propositions are orally anchored.

Johnson (2003) goes so far as to believe that there is such an important asymmetry between the verbal and the visual argument that a "visual argument", which depends on the verbal one but without reciprocity, is impossible.

In addition, according to Patterson (2010) images, which have no propositional content, cannot represent 'arguments'. A photo, he claims, does not discuss anything: it is its user who uses it to create, illustrate or emphasize a particular aspect. Moreover, what an image 'communicates' will be determined mainly by what the viewer contributes (knowledge and cultural or linguistic background).

However, Groarke (2015) noted that - since argumentation is a cognitive phenomenon - there is no theoretical reason why we cannot speak of visual argumentation. In fact, since they are cognitive or logical operations, arguments can (in principle) be expressed verbally, visually or in many other ways. Neither an image nor a verbal text is the argument itself: it is just a way of expressing or evoking arguments. It is true, of course, that visual manifestations such as images and photographs do not have the same grammar and syntax as verbal language; however, verbal language can also be ambiguous, and images - as well as other types of visual communication - have the potential to argue because they can offer a rhetorical process in which something is necessarily condensed or omitted, and consequently, it is up to the viewer to provide the unexpressed premises[136].

But we need to focus on one more, fundamental aspect. Opponents of a visual argument highlight a clear distinction between the verbal and the visual on which modern studies of visual culture, however, do not agree.

---

[136] Rational condensation in images is therefore the visual counterpart to verbal argumentation (Kjeldsen 2015).

There is a difference between words and images, of course, but we cannot exclude the discursive aspect from the visual. The study of ancient rhetoricians and the considerations made in the previous paragraph help us remember how words often evoke images, and in our perception and understanding of the visual the representations are linked and dependent on verbal concepts, without which the images would be incomprehensible. As Mitchell (2005) pointed out, all *media* are *mixed media*.

Perhaps we should also consider ancient rhetoric as a visual discipline, as an art filled with visualization, or rather, intrinsically visual. George Kennedy, in the early '70s of the last century, already put forward this perspective: since rhetoric as an art is an abstraction, and even if the concrete manifestations of this abstraction are mainly oratory and linked to the 'word', it is still possible to speak of the rhetoric of sculpture or other arts to the extent that they aim at persuasion or in any case to affect an audience.

What is therefore called a "visually based rhetorical model of communication" (Kjeldsen 2003) is quite evident in the *actio*, as well as in the *dispositio*, in the *memory*, and especially in the *elocutio* (parts all pervaded with visuality). Therefore, the speaker, after creating 'visions', will try to convey both these and 'emotions', generating the *evidentia* through detailed verbal descriptions. This will stimulate the inner eye of the audience (the *oculi mentis*), who will 'see' the events narrated by the speaker as real and vivid[137], in perfect harmony even emotionally.

---

[137] Moreover, the mind is increasingly ready to accept what it recognizes as being faithful to nature (Quint., *Inst. orat.*, VIII, 3, 71). Consequently, the speaker must create a representation that is as close to reality as possible, passing through the eyes and

It is also based on these reflections that most scholars of argumentation today recognize that visual argumentation exists and is possible[138]. This differs from ancient rhetoric where words were used to try to transmit the 'visual'. Today the 'visual' is transmitted by recognizing its molecular composition made of 'words', in a sort of coding/decoding with inverted instruments, with the 'word' as the main key[139].

4.2. Visual rhetorical tools in the American criminal trial

It is argued that lawyers and judges should keep abreast of media culture by incorporating visual technologies into their advocacy toolboxes; however, they should do so in a rigorous, ethical, and professional manner. Lawyers should develop what Ann Marie Seward Barry (1997) calls "visual intelligence", a quality of mind developed to the point of critical perceptual awareness in visual communication. It implies not only the skilled use of visual reasoning to read and communicate but also a holistic integration of skilled verbal and visual reasoning, from an understanding of how the elements that compose the meaning of images can be manipulated to distort reality, to the utilization of the visual in abstract thoughts.

Without a basic knowledge of psychology and the

---

ending up, however, by stimulating the *oculi mentis*.

[138] Regarding the recognition of visual argumentation, other modalities and sensory areas raised the interest of scholars of argumentation, in particular the sound (an argument must be represented through material modalities such as words, images or sounds): Kisicek 2014; Kisicek 2016; Groarke-Kisicek 2018.

[139] The concept of "verbal repackaging" is interesting: Groarke 2019.

principles of neuroscience regarding visual processing, lawyers will never know exactly how visual persuasion works. Lawyers and judges should be capable of identifying both conscious and unconscious processes that guide an audience's perceptual conclusions.

In order to analyze and use a visual argument in a competent and ethically correct way, lawyers also need an in-depth knowledge of the principles of visual rhetoric, an emerging discipline that draws on psychology, classical rhetoric, and media studies. Visual rhetoric analyzes how visual arguments are constructed and how images persuade; it can help lawyers to translate visual arguments into text and vice versa (Jewel 2009).

In the American legal scene, at the beginning of the millennium, a particularly relevant case in terms of visual rhetoric is certainly represented by the Skakel's[140] trial. For example, during the prosecutor's final indictment, a slide was shown that combined Skakel's audio testimony about his feeling of panic in the morning after the victim's death, the text of his testimony, and a photo of the victim's corpse; and for many commentators, the prosecution's multimedia was the decisive factor that led to a guilty verdict.

In the Skakel's appeal, his lawyers argued unsuccessfully that the State's use of selectively edited fragments of

---

[140] Michael Skakel, grandson of Ethel and Bob Kennedy, was convicted in 2002 for the brutal murder of a peer 27 years earlier. During Halloween night 1975, Martha Moxley, his neighbor, was found savagely bludgeoned to death in the bushes behind his house in Greenwich, Connecticut. Skakel was 15 years old, however he was only arrested when he reached the age of 30 and sentenced at the end of a three-week trial, in which his weakness for alcohol and drugs had emerged. However, in May 2018, the Connecticut Supreme Court surprisingly overturned what they had decided and revoked Skakel's conviction ordering a new trial.

the defendant's voice added to the victim's photos, conveyed false literal and subliminal messages to the jury and that the presentation was 'manipulative'. However, Skakel's attempt to explain the 'manipulative' nature of the prosecution's graphics did not go far enough. First of all, because the presentation of slides in the Skakel's trial was not at all 'subliminal' in the traditional meaning of the word[141]. Secondly, the slides did not contain any 'false' information.

Some scholars of American visual rhetoric (Jewel in particular) have observed that Skakel's defenders probably lacked, at least at the time, the necessary competence to evaluate and contradict the prosecutor's visual strategy.

In order to know whether an argument persuades primarily through prejudice or emotion, lawyers (and judges) need to understand the rhetorical and logical principles on which their argument is based. Knowledge of visual rhetoric will help lawyers to predict and counter opposing visual arguments effectively. For example, in the Skakel's case, the prosecutor's presentation of slides according to Jewel used emotionally powerful but analytically weak rhetorical tools. If Skakel's defense team had paid attention to deconstructing logic within the visual argument, they would have been able to isolate and attack the weaknesses and undeclared aspects of the visual argument.

There are two visual rhetorical devices commonly used in the American judicial landscape: chronological visual narratives and visual enthymeme.

In the courtroom, lawyers often employ the chronological narrative technique by juxtaposing two images of

---

[141] A truly subliminal visual presentation could flash an image so quickly that the subject would have no conscious memory of the image. This is simply because a true subliminal image flashes on a screen for 1/3,000th of a second.

the same person: the first image shows the person in a perfect and happy physical state, and the other shows the injured or dead person. Therefore, the technique emphasizes what has been taken from the victim to persuade the viewer to "do justice", both through a criminal conviction and compensation. The use of this technique in the courtroom can therefore promote emotional decision-making to the detriment of rational deliberative logic.

For example, during the final indictment for the Skakel's murder, the prosecution juxtaposed a photograph of a smiling Martha Moxley (the victim) with a photograph of her corpse.

However, the visual narrative technique can also work with a single image, plus a vivid verbal description. For example, in the Ogletree v. Graham case, the prosecutor first showed a picture of the victim with one of his children and then described the crime graphically, more than vividly[142].

Similarly, during the concluding discussion in the Gasaway v. Indiana case, a manslaughter trial, the prosecutor projected the autopsy photos of a child while reading a poem[143]. The poem began with a verbal image (of

----

[142] Ogletree v. Graham, 559 F. Supp. 2d 250, 259-260 (N.D.N.Y. 2008).

[143] "Christopher Gasaway has died;
Yes little Chris is dead.
Burned and beaten, literally,
From the soles of his feet, to the top of his head.
Pursuing one man while, yet married to another;
Kathy, lying to everyone; her husband, her sisters, her brother. When faced with devastation, running from old and rejected by new.
She struck out in rage;
Angry red turned to black and blue.
Murdered by mommy, who was entrusted to care,

"little Chris") and continued with emphasis and hearth breaking narration until the murder of the child. The prosecutor combined the reading with the images of the autopsy creating a highly emotional narrative which, according to commentators, undoubtedly influenced the jury in holding the defendant responsible[144].

However, chronological visual narratives are suggestive because they stimulate unconscious emotional reactions, which cannot be mitigated by further informative content (if any).

The visual enthymeme, instead, visually takes advantage of the characteristics of rhetorical syllogism, imposing the participation of the audience (invited to fill in the missing foundation of the argument). The undeclared premise, at the same time invisible and transparent, is natural: it is simply something that everyone knows.

The danger is that visual entities could easily rely on unconscious or implicit prejudices. Indeed, some scholars consider the visual enthymeme as an effective tool for subconscious persuasion.

After all, the unconscious acceptance of an enthymeme occurs because we generally do not stop to analyze the strength of undeclared premises; rather, we quickly accept what seems to be evidence. Therefore, the enthymeme does not create a real dialectical experience because there is no room to raise objections or refute the undeclared premises.

The Skakel's trial in the United States was a

But not one said his life would be long or his death would be fair. Christopher Gasaway has died;

Yes, little Chris is dead.

But no matter, she can always have more".

[144] Gasaway v. Indiana, 547 N.E.2d 898, 900-901 (Ind. Ct. App. 1990).

remarkable test case of visual rhetoric as used by the prosecution. The prosecution used multimedia tools throughout the trial for explanatory purposes (i.e. using images as mere media/documents). Then, in the final indictment, they proposed closing arguments combining visual images, visually displayed text, audio testimony and words. The rebuttal summation has been described as "chilling, riveting, and unforgettable".

In particular, the prosecution used a visual enthymeme leading the jurors to reconstruct a scene during which it was highlighted how the defendant had provided, in 1997 in a recording for his autobiography and in 1993 to some private investigators hired by the family, a reconstruction of that night very different from that provided to the police in 1975, just right after the crime. The prosecution highlighted these passages and contrasts, and also played the 1997 audio recording[145].

---

[145] The prosecution used Skakel's audio testimony, Martha Moxely's photographs (both dead and alive) and projected the text (in block letters) of Skakel's words to reinforce their thesis that Skakel's panicky feeling came from the fact that he had killed Martha Moxley (and not from the strong embarrassment of being caught masturbating on Moxley's property, as the defense argues). The prosecution used the audio recording along with three slides to define what Michael Skakel was thinking about the next morning when Mrs. Moxley asked if he had seen her daughter. In the first slide, the jury listens and sees the following words from Skakel's interview with the ghostwriter, who wrote his autobiography (1997). While Michael's words are being played back, a photograph of Moxley smiling and holding schoolbooks is displayed. In the second slide, the jury sees and hears the following: "Oh my God, did they see me last night? I just remember feeling panicked." For this slide, a photograph of Moxely's corpse is chosen and displayed, as found on the Moxley property. On the last slide of the visual segment, the jury sees and hears Skakel exposing his feeling of panic, and then another image of Moxley's corpse is

The enthymeme that the prosecutor used with the multimedia slides can be summarized with the following textual syllogism: a) a person who committed a murder risks panicking after realizing what he did; b) Skakel had an experience of panic the morning after Martha Moxley was murdered; c) Skakel must have killed Martha Moxley.

The visual enthymeme covered the major premise, presenting the idea that Skakel's panic was triggered by his awareness of having killed Moxley not as a plausible thesis, but as the only plausible explanation for the facts.

At first sight, the internal logic of the syllogism on which the visual enthymeme was based seems to be correct. However, a closer look reveals serious weaknesses within the syllogism because there are other possible convincing premises, namely explanations of why Skakel panicked the day after Moxley's murder. Overcoming the major premise, the enthymeme has not allowed to investigate its logical structure, in fact leaving no room for alternative explanations for Skakel's feeling of panic.

Unlike the assessment made by Skakel's defense team and supported on appeal, the prosecution's defense and visual argumentation was not false or subliminal, but there is no doubt that a logical leap was favored in the jurors (as to whether Skakel's feeling of panic was because he had committed murder). In addition, the photographs of Moxley's corpse may undoubtedly have generated rather quick and unconscious feelings of fear, which may have further contributed to the conviction of Skakel's jury.

---

shown. At the end of the audio-visual segment, the prosecutor asks: "Could the sight of Dorothy Moxley's corpse produce a feeling of panic in an innocent person, in a person who had gone to sleep without knowing anything about Martha Moxley's murder?".

4.3. Visual rhetorical devices in the Italian criminal trial

The Skakel's case has therefore raised important ethical and professional issues concerning visual arguments. It is questionable whether similar considerations can be made in the Italian legal field.

In Italy (and not only there) it is necessary to distinguish between cases in which the decision is entrusted to a single judge, a panel of judges, or a court supplemented by six lay judges (Court of Assizes) - (according to the importance of the case). It is easy to understand how the management of visual tools in front of a court composed mostly of common citizens can lead to very different evaluations and strategic choices, also in terms of visual arguments, compared to the purely technical context of a trial without jurors and audience.

It is frequent, especially from the public prosecution, the use of multimedia supports and re-enactment - in a simplified form and with audio and visual elements - of fundamental elements of the accusatory thesis.

There is an Italian legal case (the trial of Amanda Knox and Raffaele Sollecito for the death of Meredith Kercher) particularly followed also by American scholars, who had the opportunity to see the role played, in the first instance, by the use by the prosecution (prosecutor Giuliano Mignini) of a computer-generated simulation. This showed an *avatar* (Amanda) killing another *avatar* (Meredith) and ended with a bloody photo of the crime scene and Kercher's body. The animation turned out to be an animated version of the prosecution's thesis that saw Amanda Knox in the role of a sexy *femme fatale*, "Foxy Knoxy", as the British tabloids called her; a "She-Devil", as many European journalists have written, using a phrase from the prosecutor.

Sherwin observed how prosecutors and lawyers activate the popular imagination through the use of well-known characters ("She-Devil", "*femme fatale*") and build scripts (in the Kercher's case, a never-before-seen "sex game gone wrong") to help frame their 'story' in court. And, increasingly often, "their advocacy begins well before the courtroom doors open" (Sherwin, 2011). A trial started before and outside the courtrooms.

A narrative frame is set, which should reflect a belief system that is easy for the audience to accept. A frame within which dissonant details are removed. It is difficult to reconstruct past events in greater detail; but with a recognizable story frame and a cast of familiar characters, they can convince their audience (jurors and judges alike[146]) to fill in the missing details: "This is how this kind of story goes", "That is how this kind of person behaves" (Sherwin 2011).

In the construction of this frame, graphics and digital animationshave a fundamental role, because they can accompany those who have to judge anywhere and at any time, on the crime scene as on the one before it, offering a subjective visual narrative.

Video and animation are therefore undoubtedly powerful tools, even on the judicial stage; but a visual tool is still the result of a choice: it is a 'camera' that frames a single point of view, a subjective one. Therefore, one can never disregard the analysis of its real bases.

---

[146] It is frequent, however, that the use of visual tools, even by the public prosecution in Italy, is aimed at creating a fascinating setting also for exclusively technical listeners. The practical exhibition, for example, of instruments used for the commission of the crime (and which, if not seen, could not make one think of their capacity to offend), the visualization of crude images of the victim and of the crime scene, the listening of well isolated audio fragments of the victim or of the defendant, are frequent.

When the judge and jury of the Kercher's trial - Sherwin asked himself - watched the prosecution's animation video at the Amanda Knox murder trial, whose fantasy did they enter? (Sherwin 2011).

This is not always visual argumentation, but mere recourse to the visual to charm even an exclusively technical (but still human) audience. The risk, not to be underestimated, is that this exasperated (and sometimes desperate) use of visual tools allows the operators (especially the prosecution) to disregard "reasonable doubts". Visual tools cannot allow operators to construct a parallel world, in which everything is possible, a *docu-fiction* free from the principles of the judicial system to which they belong, and the ethics that oversees it and its interpreters.

4.4. Limitations and problems of visual rhetoric. Concluding remarks

The integration of visual components into judicial arguments has undoubtedly brought many benefits. The images help to make the messages captivating, to favor their comprehension, and they are particularly useful in an age of inadequate listening skills, where it is necessary to fight boredom and to deal with impulses very different from the textual ones.

Visual arguments provide a message in a multimodal way, which is the way in recent years we have become accustomed to receiving and processing information.

It would be unwise, however, to ignore the many problems that exist within visual tools. Visual reasoning is not only fallible, it is also based on an abstract set of rules that do not follow the rational principles of logic. When we visualize visual information, we are rather susceptible to making judgments too quickly, unconsciously, or based on automatic emotional processes. Moreover, when we see something persuasive, we do not tend to ask questions about the underlying logic. We tend to believe that what we see is true and correct.

Adaptation to contemporary ways of communication must go hand in hand with maintaining the credibility of our judicial systems; and this will require the development of much more refined skills for a critical visual judgment.

One can therefore also agree on the argumentative possibilities of the visual tools, but its use must, first of all, presuppose operators who are adequately trained and therefore able to value and use rhetorical thoughts, which can generate an argumentatively well-founded 'visual', accompanied by the word that makes itself image (according to the teaching of Quintilian and his predecessors).

Otherwise, we will have only a sterile jubilation of images without words, like a beauty without intellect; and with the real risk of being dramatically trapped by them.

REFERENCES

Classics

Cicerone Marco Tullio, *Opere retoriche*, a cura di G. Norcio, UTET, Torino, 1976

Cornifici Rhetorica ad C. Herennium, a cura di G. Calboli, Pàtron, Bologna, 1969

Quintiliano Marco Fabio, *L'istituzione oratoria*, a cura di R. Faranda e P. Pecchiura, UTET, Torino, 1979

Vico G., *Institutiones oratoriae*, a cura di G. Crifò, Istituto Suor Orsola Benincasa, Napoli, 1989

Dictionaries

DEI I - Dizionario etimologico della lingua italiana, a cura di M. Cortellazzo, P. Zolli, Zanichelli, Bologna, 1979-1988

Dizionario di linguistica, a cura di J. Dubois, L. Guespin, Ch. E J. B. Marcellesi, J. P. Mével, Zanichelli, Bologna, 1979

Dizionario di linguistica e di filologia, metrica, retorica, a cura di G. L. Beccaria, Einaudi, Torino, 2004

Dizionario di retorica. Con elementi di linguistica, fonetica, stilistica e narratologia per l'oratore quotidiano, a cura di G. Spòsito, Intra, 2020

Dizionario di retorica e stilistica, UTET, Torino, 1995

Grande Dizionario Italiano dell'uso, a cura di T. De Mauro, UTET, Torino, 1999

Books and papers

Alexy R., *A Theory of Legal Argumentation: the Theory of Rational Discourse as Theory of Legal Justification*, Clarendon Press - Oxford University Press, New York-Oxford, 1989

Arato FF., *Parola di avvocato. L'eloquenza forense in Italia tra Cinque e Ottocento*, Giappichelli, Torino, 2015

Barthes R., *Rhétorique de l'image*, in *Communications*, 4, 1964, 40

Barthes R., *La retorica antica*, Bompiani, Milano, 1972

Bellodi Ansaloni A., *L'arte dell'avvocato, actor veritatis. Studi di retorica e deontologia forense*, BUP, Bologna, 2011

Bellodi Ansaloni A., *Scienza giuridica e retorica forense*, Maggioli, Rimini, 2017

Benzi M., *Il problema logico delle fallacie*, in Mucciarelli G. - Celani G. (a cura di), *Quando il pensiero sbaglia. La fallacia tra psicologia e scienza*, UTET, Torino, 2002

Bernardo A., *Le fallacie argomentative nella formazione del giurista*, in *Cultura e diritti*, 2015, 15

Bobbio N., *Il linguaggio del diritto*, Giuffrè, Milano, 1994

Calamandrei P., *Elogio dei giudici scritto da un avvocato*, Le Monnier, Firenze, 1954

Calboli Montefusco L., *La teoria degli status causarum nella retorica greca e romana*, Olms-Weidmann, Hilldesheim-Zurich-New York, 1986

Calboli Montefusco L., Exordium Narratio Epilogus. *Studi sulla teoria retorica greca e romana delle parti del discorso*, CLUEB, Bologna, 1988

Calboli Montefusco L., *Logica, retorica e giurisprudenza nella dottrina degli status*, in Mantovani D. (a cura di), *Per la storia del pensiero giuridico romano: dall'età dei pontefici alla scuola di Servio. Atti del Seminario di S. Marino, 7-9 gennaio 1993*, UTET, Torino, 1996

Carofiglio G., *La regola dell'equilibrio*, Einaudi, Torino, 2014

Cattani A., *Discorsi ingannevoli. Argomenti per difendersi, attaccare, divertirsi*, GB, Padova, 1995

Cattani A. et al. (a cura di), *La svolta argomentativa. 50 anni dopo Perelman e Toulmin*, Loffredo, Napoli, 2009

Cattani A., De Conti M. (a cura di), *Didattica, dibattito, fallacie e altri campi dell'argomentazione*, Loffredo, Napoli, 2012

Cavalla F., *A proposito della ricerca della verità nel processo*, in *Verifiche* 13 (1984), 469

Cavalla F., voce *Topica giuridica*, in *Enciclopedia del Diritto*, XLIV, Giuffrè, Milano, 1992, 720

Cavalla F. (a cura di), *Retorica Processo Verità. Principi di filosofia forense*, FrancoAngeli, Milano, 2007

Classen C. J., *Diritto, retorica, politica. La strategia retorica di Cicerone*, il Mulino, Bologna, 1998 (1985)

Conte G., *Il linguaggio della difesa civile, in Lingua e Diritto. Scritto e parlato nelle professioni legali. Atti del convegno organizzato dall'Accademia della Crusca e dalla Scuola Superiore dell'Avvocatura (Firenze, 9 marzo 2012)*, a cura di A. Mariani Marini e F. Bambi, Pisa University Press, Pisa, 2013, 35

Copi Irving M., Cohen C., *Introduzione alla logica*, Il Mulino, Bologna, 1997

Dell'Anna M. V., *Fra attori e convenuti. Lingua dell'avvocato e lingua del giudice nel processo civile, in Lingua e processo. Le parole del diritto di fronte al giudice*, a cura di F. Bambi, Accademia della Crusca, Firenze, 2017, 57

Dell'Anna M. V., *Fra attori e convenuti. Lingua dell'avvocato e lingua del giudice nel processo civile*, in *Lingua e processo. Le parole del diritto di fronte al giudice*, a cura di F. Bambi, Accademia della Crusca, Firenze, 2016, 57

Dupont F., *Teatro e società a Roma*, Laterza, Roma-Bari, 1991 (1985)

Eco U., *Semiotica e filosofia del linguaggio*, Einaudi, Torino, 1984

Ellero M. P., *Retorica. Guida all'argomentazione e alle figure del discorso*, Carocci, Roma, 2017

Eemeren F. H. Van, Grootendorst R., *Argumentation, Communication, and Fallacies. A Pragma-dialectical Perspective*, Lawrence Erlbaum Associates, Hillsdale N. J., 1992

Eemeren F. H. Van et al., *Fundamentals of Argumentation Theory. A Handbook of Historical Backgrounds and Contemporary Developments*, Lawrence Erlbaum Associates, Mahwah N.J., 1996

Farau S., Farau M., *Il linguaggio forense nel tempo*, in CEPIG, 1985, 49

Fontanier P., *Les figures du discours*, Flammarion, Paris, 1977 (1827)

Fumaroli M., *L'età dell'eloquenza*, Adelphi, Milano, 2002 (1980)

Gianformaggio L., voce *Topica*, in *Grande Dizionario Enciclopedico*, XVIII, UTET, Torino, 1973, 906

Giliberti G., *Elementi di storia del diritto romano*, Giappichelli, Torino, 2001

Giuliani A., voce *Logica del diritto (teoria dell'argomentazione)*, in *Enciclopedia del Diritto*, XXV, Giuffrè, Milano, 1975, 13

Giuliani A., *Prova e convincimento. Profili logici e storici*, in *Quaderni*, 1997, 235

Grice H. P., *Logica e conversazione*, il Mulino, Bologna, 1993 (1989)

Groarke L., *Going Multimodal: What is a Mode of Arguing and Why Does it Matter?*, in *Argumentation*, 29, 2015, 133

Groarke L. – Kisicek G., *Sound Arguments: An Introduction To Auditory Argument*, in *Argumentation and Inference*, a cura di S. Oswald – M. Didier, College Publications, London, 2018, 117

Groarke L., *On Dove, Visual Evidence and Verbal Repackaging*, in *OSSA Conference Archive*, 10, 2019, 1

Gruppo μ, *Retorica generale. Le figure della comunicazione*, Bompiani, Milano, 1976 (1970)

Gulotta G. (a cura di), *Trattato di psicologia giudiziaria*, Giuffè, Milano, 1987

Jacobson R., *Saggi di linguistica generale*, Feltrinelli, Milano, 1983 (1963)

Jewel L. A., *Through a Glass Darkly: Using Brain Science and Visual Rhetoric to Gain a Professional Perspective on Visual Advocacy*, in *Southern California Interdisciplinary Law Journal*, 2009, 237

Johnson R. H., *Why "Visual Arguments" aren't Arguments?*, in *Informal Logic at 25, Proceedings of the Windsor Conference*, H. V. Hansen - J. C. Tindale – A. Blair – R. H. Johnson (ed.), *Ontario Society for the Study of Argumentation (OSSA)*, Windsor, 2003, 1

Kennedy, *The Art of Persuasion in Greece*, Princeton University Press, Princeton, 1970

Kennedy, *The Art Thetoric in the Roman World*, Princeton University Press, Princeton, 1972

Kennedy, *A New History of Classical Rhetoric*, Princeton University Press, Princeton, 1994

Kisicek G., *The Role of Prosodic Features in the Analysis of Multimodal Argumentation*, in *Proceedings of the 8th International Conference of the International Society for the Study of Argumentation*, B. Garssen - D. Godden - G. Mitchell - F. Snoek Henkemas (ed.), Sic Sat, Amsterdam, 2014, 730

Kisicek G., *Prosodic Features in the Analysis of Multimodal Argumentation*, in *Argumentation and Reasoned Action*, D. Mohamed - M. Lewinski (ed.), College Publications, Milton Keynes, 2016, 629

Kjeldsen J. E., *Talking to the Eye: Visuality in Ancient Rhetoric*, in *World & Image*, 19, 2003, 133

Kjeldsen J. E., *The Rhetoric of Thick Representation: How Pictures Render the Importance and Strength of an Argument Salient*, in *Argumentation*, 29, 2015, 19

Kjeldsen J. E., *The Rhetoric of Sound, the Sound of Arguments. Three Propositions, Three Questions, and an After-thought for the Study of Sonic and Multimodal Argumentation*, in *Argumentation and Advocacy*, 2018

Lausberg H., *Elementi di retorica*, il Mulino, Bologna, 1969 (1949)

Mitchell W. J. T., *There Are no Visual Media*, in *Journal of Visual Culture*, 4, 2005, 257

Moro P., *L'argomentazione forense come difesa della parte e persuasione del giudice*, in *Cultura e diritti*, 2015, 25

Moro P., *L'Arte della scrittura giuridica. Retorica e testo difensivo*, Libreria Al Segno Editrice, Padova, 2016

Moro P., *Didattica e retorica forense*, in *Cultura e diritti*, 2018, 33

Mortara Garavelli B., *Manuale di retorica*, Bompiani, Milano, 2019 (1988)

Mortara Garavelli B., *Le parole e la giustizia. Divagazioni grammaticali e retoriche su testi giuridici italiani*, Einaudi, Torino, 2001

Mortara Garavelli B., *L'oratoria forense: tradizione e regole*, in *L'avvocato e il processo. Le tecniche della difesa*, a cura di A. Mariani Marini e M. Paganelli, Giuffrè, Milano, 2003, 69

Mortara Garavelli B., *Il parlar figurato. Manualetto di figure retoriche*, Laterza, Roma-Bari, 2010

Patterson S. W., *A Picture Held us Captive: The Later Wittgenstein on Visual Argumentation*, in *Cogency*, 2, 2010, 122

Perelman C., *Logica giuridica e nuova retorica*, Giuffrè, Milano, 1979 (1976)

Perelman C., *Il dominio retorico*, Einaudi, Torino, 1981 (1977)

Perelman C., Olbrechts-Tyteca L., *Trattato dell'argomentazione. La nuova retorica*, Einaudi, Torino, 1966 (1958)

Piattelli Palmarini M., *L'arte di persuadere. Come impararla, come esercitarla, come difendersene*, Mondadori, Milano, 1995

Pierantoni A., *Gli avvocati di Roma antica*, Zanichelli, Bologna 1900

Plebe A., *Breve storia della retorica antica*, Laterza, Roma-Bari, 1988 (1961)

Plebe A., Emanuele P., *Manuale di retorica*, Laterza, Roma-Bari, 1988

Preti H., *Retorica e logica. Le due culture*, Einaudi, Torino, 1968

Puppo F., *Dalla vaghezza del linguaggio alla retorica forense. Saggio di logica giuridica*, CEDAM, Padova, 2012

Raimondi E., *La retorica d'oggi*, il Mulino, Bologna, 2002

Reboul O., *Introduzione alla retorica*, il Mulino, Bologna, 1996 (1994)

Rigotti F., *La verità retorica. Etica, conoscenza, persuasione*, Feltrinelli, Milano, 1995

Sagnotti S. C., *Retorica e logica. Aristotele, Cicerone, Quintiliano, Vico*, Giappichelli, Torino, 1999

Schopenauer A., *L'arte di ottenere ragione esposta in 38 stratagemmi*, Adelphi, Milano, 1991 (1830)

Seward Barry A. M., *Visual Intelligence. Perception, Image, and Manipulation in Visual Communication*, Suny Press, 1997, 9

Sherwin R. K., *The Digital Trial*, in *Culture & Society*, october 12 2011

Sherwin R. K., *Visual Literacy for the Legal Profession*, in *European Journal of Legal Education*, November 2018, 7

Smith A., *Lezioni di retorica e belle lettere*, Quattroventi, Urbino, 1993

Sposito G., *Il luogo dell'oratore. Argomentazione topica e retorica forense in Cicerone*, ESI, Napoli, 2001

Sposito G., *Assurdo e ridicolo. Ironia e* deductio ad absurdum *nella retorica forense*, in *Cultura giuridica e diritto vivente*, 5, 2018

Sposito G., "Visiones". Visual tools *nell'oratoria forense antica e moderna*, in *Cultura giuridica e diritto vivente*, 6, 2019

Sposito G., *Quanto siamo retorici. Libera l'oratore che è in te*, Intra, 2020

Stolfi E., *Gli attrezzi del giurista. Introduzione alle pratiche discorsive del diritto*, Giappichelli, Torino, 2018

Toulmin S., *Gli usi dell'argomentazione*, Rosenberg & Sellier, Torino, 1975 (1958)

Traversi A., *Arte della persuasione e processo*, Giuffrè, Milano, 1998

Traversi A., *La difesa penale. Tecniche argomentative e oratorie*, Giuffrè, Milano, 2014

Vickers B, *Storia della retorica*, il Mulino, Bologna, 1994 (1989)

Viehweg T., *Topica e giurisprudenza*, Giuffè, Milano, 1962 (1953)

Vincenti U., *Metodologia giuridica*, Cedam, Padova, 2008

Woods J., Irvine A., Walton D., *Argument: critical Thinking. Logic and the Fallacies*, Prentice Hall, Toronto, 2000

SUMMARY

9 791280 035059